Fooled by Early Adopters

Fooled by Early Adopters

A Leadership Fable for Founders Trying to Scale

Jeff Eversmann

with Kathryn Eversmann

First paperback edition November 2022

ISBN 979-8-218-00331-9 (paperback)

Published by Kindle Direct Publishing
www.jeffeversmann.com

Cover image: iStock illustration ID:960303126

for Vaughn

CONTENTS

FOREWORD

We live in a time where it is easier than ever to create a technology startup, but still only a fraction succeed. This incredibly high level of failure can be attributed to many things, but mostly it comes from a fundamental misunderstanding of what matters in the earliest stages of a startup.

Technology has opened many possibilities for founders; digital platforms, automation, and globalization allow new companies to scale like never before. The possibilities for exponential growth are very real and exciting. The downside, however, is that the current system prioritizes the focus on developing the product, brute forcing sales, and then attempting to scale. This is where founders can quickly set themselves up for failure.

You might be thinking, *What's wrong with this approach? Attempting to scale is the whole point, right?*

Yes, it is. But it doesn't work like that.

First, you need customers. There is no business without customers. Customers do not care about your great ideas and your grand plans. They buy what fits them, what solves their problems. Understanding customers, then, supersedes all other tasks in the early stages of a startup.

I work as a strategist and consultant for early-stage high-growth founders. Since 2014, I've had the opportunity to work with over 300 startups, training founders to model and design their business, see and understand the assumptions they have, experiment and validate to get grounded in reality about their customers and their market, and craft and improve their offer to achieve early traction. After struggling with many cases, I noticed some essential elements were missing from the general approach, and even seasoned CEOs struggled because of an incomplete early-stage mindset. Over time I developed a more comprehensive approach, one that integrates customer development, business modeling, core market strategy, systems thinking, design thinking, game thinking, and advanced lean methodology into a framework to design the venture and systematically make progress in reaching product/market fit.

In the process, I've spent time one-on-one with founders who experienced all kinds of barriers to growth, but it often comes down to the same issue: understanding customers. Without this, there is nothing to build on. In this book, Jeff addresses the importance of understanding your customers and something else that might be just as important: learning *how* to be a founder.

Being a founder takes more than having a good idea. Many founders have good ideas. Becoming an effective founder is about continuing to have ideas – over and over and over again. It's about knowing the right questions to ask yourself and your team. All too often, founders struggle when they get lost in uncertainty and the realization that they don't have all the answers. It is essential to know that that is okay. When you are early, you won't have all the answers. Being a founder is about the search. As Steve Blank wrote, "A startup is a temporary organization designed to search for a repeatable and scalable business model." The entire job of the founder is to search.

Jeff understands the search and the importance of asking questions. With years of experience at startups in different stages and roles, he clearly understands these struggles inside and out.

Fooled by Early Adopters addresses a central issue for startup founders, possibly resulting in the most uncertainty: how to allocate scarce resources to reach product/market fit. It would be impossible to create a step-by-step guide to success when it comes to this because different business models need different steps, but Jeff takes a different approach. He focuses not on the "what" of all the steps but on the "how." He shows founders communicating and strategizing with their team to know when things are going in the right direction and when it's time to shift gears.

This book is unique for its multi-faceted approach to helping founders understand themselves and their businesses. It's fantastic for wrapping it into an engaging story rather than reading like a textbook. As I read this book, I saw myself in the characters and scratched out a few notes inspired by the dialogue and the story. As you read, you might find yourself motivated to take on a new approach to understanding your customers or unexpectedly excited to talk with your team, call your coach, or, for some of you, finally get started on your startup.

I hope you do. Life is too short not to act on your dreams.

And don't forget to talk to your customers. Seriously, Jeff is right. Listening saves a lot of time.

Ada Ryland
Ada Ryland Consulting
www.adaryland.com

1
FIRE THE VP

"I think I need to replace my VP of Sales," Jonathan said as he sat down for lunch.

"That was quick," Vaughn replied, eyes a little wide. And then he shook his head and smiled. "I figured we could at least order lunch before we jumped into talking about work."

And maybe it had been a little hasty. Jonathan had barely even acknowledged his surroundings, only for the couple of seconds it took to find Vaughn at their table. He sat back in his chair for a second. The two of them were in the nicest part of the restaurant, seated out on the patio but shaded from the sunshine. The view over the railing managed to contain both the city skyline and Coronado Island right next to it—if he listened, he could hear the waves hitting the rocks below them.

Jonathan realized with a little bit of guilt that it was exactly the sort of business lunch he'd dreamed about when he first moved to Southern California. His dreams just hadn't included his company's failure to achieve its goals.

"I'm sorry," he said. "You're right. Since we missed our sales forecast for the second quarter in a row, I thought I should suggest some possible changes before you tell me the board is asking me to step down."

Jonathan was anxious about the fact that Vaughn had invited him to lunch today, and he knew he wasn't hiding it very well. Vaughn was a long-time mentor and the largest investor in SyncAnalytix, but he didn't hear from him very often outside of board meetings unless it was a spontaneous invitation for dinner or coffee (or, once, a weekend skiing in Aspen). Lunch invitations made a whole week in advance weren't usually a part of their routine.

Jonathan, on the other hand, was a rising star in the field of data analytics and Internet-of-Things (IoT)[1]. He had started his career in Silicon Valley during the dot-com period, quickly rose through the engineering ranks, and ended up responsible for a $20-million development budget before he was 26. When the bubble burst, he moved his family to Southern California where he enrolled in an MBA program at USC. By 30, he was back into technology startups as a co-founder of BlackBee, one of the first implementers of the ZigBee® standard. Selling BlackBee put him on the radar of local investors, and all of a sudden people were using the name *Jonathan Reeves* and *entrepreneur* in the same sentence.

The common growing pains in the startup world waited to hit Jonathan until his second time around, after he'd founded SyncAnalytix. He was determined to figure out what wasn't working within the company as soon as he could, but he knew it was just a matter of time before the Board of Directors noticed that he was falling short.

"Whoa, whoa, where did that come from?" Vaughn held his hands up, trying to defuse the tension. "That's not why I wanted to meet for lunch. Take a breath."

Jonathan let out the breath he didn't know he'd been holding.

Vaughn continued, "If anything, this is a pep-talk. Nobody on the board has been talking about asking you to step down. It's the

---

[1] Definitions, references, and additional resources can be found in the Notes chapter at the end of the book.

opposite, actually. We can see you're in a tough spot. I scheduled this lunch to ask if there's anything we can do to help."

Vaughn was the Chairman of the SyncAnalytix Board of Directors, a role he had held since leading the Series A investment. Two things were unique about his position with SyncAnalytix. He didn't usually lead investments in startups where he had a personal relationship with the founder—but the opportunity had intrigued him, and the investment passed diligence with flying colors. Additionally, Vaughn tended to only make angel investments alone. This time was different; he had decided to pull together a syndicate of co-investors in order to set the terms and garner a board seat.

"Okay. That's a relief," Jonathan replied tentatively, and looked back down at his menu. "Things have been crazy since the last board meeting. I missed another dance recital and had to pull out of a camping trip I was supposed to go on with my son's troop. I thought the extra time at work would help, but it still feels like we're building the bridge we're walking on."

"Let's take a break from talking about it altogether then," Vaughn offered as he motioned to the waiter that they were ready to order.

The two men ordered their lunch and managed to avoid talking about business over the next 30 minutes. Jonathan brought Vaughn up to date on the latest with his family, the new puppy they had recently adopted, and the status of his Charger rebuild.

If a new puppy was any indication that Jonathan tended to overcommit during times of stress, purchasing a Charger police cruiser from auction was just another crazy idea in a long list of attempts to have a *hobby*. And that was on top of the mindfulness workshop series his wife had signed him up for—probably with the hope that he would be inspired to pull back from one or more of those commitments and be more present with his family. Sitting at lunch that afternoon, he realized that it definitely sounded like way too much when he said it all out loud.

Vaughn, always capable of switching between intensity and lightheartedness, kept the conversation more relaxed to avoid triggering Jonathan's anxiety again over the situation at SyncAnalytix. He engaged Jonathan on his activities outside of the office and managed to prevent him a few times from circling back to work. He talked about his most recent trip to the Galápagos Islands and the sailing charter he took to get there. Vaughn was a great storyteller and conversationalist, regardless of the topic, and the recounting of his sailing experience filled their table with laughter.

As their lunch was drawing to a close, he brought the conversation back around to where Jonathan had started.

"So..." he let out a long breath, leaning back into his chair and abandoning his empty plate in favor of his iced tea. "Tell me about this VP thing. Why do you think it's time to replace Alex? He hasn't been around for very long, at this point, has he?"

Jonathan nodded. He'd hired Alex less than a year ago.

"I thought Alex was going to be great, but it seems like things aren't where they should be with sales. When we hired him ten months ago, he had the right experience and said all the right things, but the results just aren't... right, I guess." Jonathan felt more relaxed than when they first sat down at the restaurant and could manage a more professional tone this time. If he'd had to explain what was going on with Alex half an hour ago, he would have ended up rambling.

"I could tell in yesterday's board meeting that you seemed a little embarrassed by the Sales report," Vaughn said. "I agree, when I met with Alex during the interview process, I thought he would be a great addition to the team. To be honest, though, I've been through this phase with other entrepreneurs, and I'm not surprised by your current situation."

"Not surprised?" Jonathan repeated to himself. His brow furrowed. He cleared his throat. "So, you think everything is on track even though we missed our forecast for the second quarter in a row?"

"Well, I'm not surprised, but I wouldn't say 'everything is on track.' I was actually hoping we could sit down and talk about what 'track' we're on." Vaughn's true agenda for this lunch meeting was beginning to surface, and it renewed Jonathan's insecurity that there was something the board saw that he didn't.

"That's where I'm stuck," Jonathan said thoughtfully. "Shouldn't the sales effort be *led* by the VP of Sales? I thought when we hired Alex, he would come in and take charge of the Sales Department so I could go back to focusing on the product."

He shifted in his chair. "I know that, ultimately, I'm responsible, but sales is not my expertise, so I really don't know how to tell Alex to do his job. I just know that I don't feel good about where we're at."

Vaughn nodded, considering the thoughts Jonathan had just shared in the past few minutes.

"You're right that you, as the CEO, are ultimately responsible for sales, just as you're responsible for the success of your other direct reports."

Vaughn was careful with his next words. "So, what are you doing to help Alex be successful?"

"In what way do you mean?" Jonathan asked. "We give Alex the funding and the resources he needs, and he has the full support of Marketing and Engineering. Everyone knows sales is our priority. We have a product, we have customers, now it's time to scale the business. What am I missing?"

"Is it the right time to scale?" Vaughn asked.

Jonathan shook his head and blinked his eyes.

"Of course," he protested. "Any time is the right time to scale."

Vaughn didn't respond right away. He finally spoke up again when it appeared that Jonathan had nothing more to add.

"How would you define when it's the 'right time to scale?'"

"I can't imagine I would propose another time to scale the company," Jonathan responded. "Everyone knows that as soon as you've launched an MVP, it's time to scale. I mean, isn't that why we did Series A— to raise money to fuel sales and marketing?"

"Jon, that's exactly why we funded Series A." Vaughn encouraged Jonathan. "But fueling sales and marketing takes more than just selling. Customer discovery focuses on *identifying* the customer's needs, not just *selling* to the customer."

Vaughn caught the attention of the waiter and smiled, gesturing for him to bring the check.

Then he turned and looked directly at Jonathan, "I'd like you to go to an event a friend of mine is speaking at next week. She's an executive coach and I think you'd get a lot out of meeting her."

"Is she an expert on scaling companies?"

"She's doing a talk on Conversational Intelligence®," Vaughn replied as he paid the check. "You can txt Hannah to get the specific details."

Jonathan paused. "What does that have to do with our sales issue?"

"I don't think sales is the issue. It sounds more like the problem is timing. Conversational Intelligence could be a good tool for you to use with your team to figure out what the issue is. And, of course,

I want you to meet my friend, Helen," Vaughn said as they got up from the table. "We'll talk more later. Give my best to Margot and the kids."

As Jonathan drove back to the office, he thought more about the question posed by Vaughn:

Why is now not the right time to scale? and

If not now, is this Helen person going to be able to tell me when?

2
FORECAST REVIEW

"Maria, how was your hiking trip this weekend?" Alex asked, trying to ease into the forecast review. Breaking the ice was always a little more complicated with his team scattered across different cities. Still, he preferred to take the weekly call in the conference room even though everyone else was calling in from outside the office.

"Beautiful, but I think I might have overdone it," Maria responded. "My calves are killing me this morning, and I somehow ended up with blisters everywhere."

"Well, I envy you," Alex added. "The closest I got to nature this weekend was standing at the edge of my balcony. I don't envy the blisters though."

"I'll take blisters any day if it means I get to keep living out here. But what about your big city weekend?"

"Ha! Non-eventful," Alex replied. "Since the last board meeting, I basically worked the whole weekend trying to get our sales numbers back on track."

"Well, I have some good news to report this morning," Maria's voice took on a more cheerful tone, no doubt in response to hearing about Alex's weekend spent working. "But I don't want to jumpstart the meeting before Mark joins the call. Is he the only one missing?"

"I just sent a reminder. He should be joining soon. It'll just be the three of us."

Sometimes Jonathan joined the forecast review meetings, too, but he tended to take things off track with highly technical questions. Alex had decided soon after he took on the role of Sales VP that it was better to include Jonathan in the pipeline meetings, when there was more open discussion about how the product might need to change to go after specific opportunities.

"Sorry I'm late," Mark chimed in after he joined the call. "Customer call ran over."

Alex doubted that was the case since Mark was on the West Coast and had probably just started his workday. In the interest of time, though, he made a note to address Mark's punctuality in their next one-on-one.

"Let's get started," Alex said, after shifting to a more formalized tone to start the meeting. He thought briefly about mentioning the board's disappointment that the Sales Team had missed the forecast again but decided to focus on the positive.

"Maria, can you go first, since you said you might have some encouraging news for us?"

"Sure. It may not be as encouraging as we would like, but I had a call with my contact at Brexar on Thursday and I think we can get that project moving again. As you probably remember, they went on-hold because they were looking at moving out of oil field monitoring. I think they thought they could sell the division, but they never said who the buyer might be. Anyway, that deal is off the table, which means we're back in the mix."

SyncAnalytix software provided sophisticated machine learning algorithms for IOT that could be used to detect anomalies and project future trends. Some of the early wins came in the oil & gas industry and from customers that Jonathan knew personally from BlackBee.

"Do we still have the technical win and business win on this one?" Alex asked.

"Yes, nothing has changed there, in fact, our fit might have increased because they had a sensor go down at one of their installations and no one knew the pipe was leaking for almost six hours. With our real-time monitoring, they would have known instantly that the sensor performance was down and could have had it replaced before the leak happened."

"I would say technically that's good news," Alex said. "What's the next step?"

"They had some turnover in procurement since we were in there before, so I need to connect with the new procurement person and update the proposal."

"Do you need anything from me, or are we just updating the dates and re-submitting?"

"I think just dates and resubmitting," Maria replied. "Unless you want to increase the price or change to a perpetual license. The recent sensor failure and leak cost them a lot of money. Makes me think our solution might be priced too low."

"We might be leaving money on the table, but we really need to get some deals closed," Alex insisted. "On top of that, I don't want Brexar to think we're taking advantage of the situation."

"Fair enough," Maria said. "Anyway, that's my big news. Everything else is just business as usual. I hope to move a few prospects to the next stage this week, scheduling demos and stuff. Oh, and I might be getting on a plane to visit Rally Pipe in Minneapolis, but that hasn't been confirmed yet."

"I appreciate your persistence! And I'm glad to hear Brexar is a possibility again. I have a few thoughts on Rally Pipe, but we don't have too much time today, so let's switch over to Mark."

There was an awkward silence on the line while Alex and Maria waited for Mark to chime in with an update on his forecast.

"Mark, are you still there?" Alex asked.

A few seconds later Mark spoke up. "Sorry, I was talking away and didn't realize that my phone was on mute. Anyway, I can't top Maria's update, but I think I've made some progress at Dane Security. They are still wanting us to get more competitive on price, but I found out why."

"Dane is where your friend works, right? Or an old coworker?" Alex asked.

"Coworker," Mark confirmed. "Liam and I worked together for a few years before he went to Dane. Anyway, he told me this week that they're also looking at other options to grow revenue. So, if we can get our price lower, then the business is ours."

"This is the licensing deal we're talking about?" Alex started, "If I remember right, Dane is thinking they could grow their value-added reseller business by including our IoT solution with their security offering."

"That's the one. Liam and I came up with the idea over beers three months ago—I think in Seattle—but I can't remember," Mark laughed. "Anyway, he ran it up the management chain and got buy-in from the powers that be. We almost closed the deal, but when the proposal went across the CFO's desk, he asked what competitors were offering."

"Let's bring it up with Jonathan during the pipeline meeting later this week," Alex decided. "I don't think we understand the problem and use-case well enough to get more aggressive on pricing."

"If we can drop our pricing, I can close the deal Friday when I'm up in Seattle again," Mark added.

"We'll know more Wednesday. What other projects do you have going on this week?" Alex asked.

"No other deals in the works," Mark said, "but lots of activity. Sacramento today, Portland on Tuesday, and then heading to Chicago for two days on Wednesday."

"Chicago?" Maria asked.

The Sales Team was small at SyncAnalytix, and account executives were assigned wide territories. There was some discussion about switching to an industry vertical assignment, but so far, no conflicts had occurred over who should get a particular customer, so regional-focused seemed just as good as vertical-focused. There just weren't many customers to begin with. Organic and paid leads were few, and most opportunities came from each account executive's personal network.

"You bet, there's a security conference going on and a lot of my contacts will be there," he said. "Don't worry, if I come across any opportunities in your territory, I'll send them your way. This conference is mostly for reconnecting with some people I know in the security space to see if I can drum up any leads."

"All security stuff this week?" Alex asked.

"Yeah," Mark answered. "I really think we can make our stuff work in the security space. Might not be as important to security as it is to oil & gas, but with my connections, I can get people looking at it."

Alex had a sinking feeling that going after the security market right now would be a distraction. With only one marketing person, it was hard to produce the necessary collateral to support two verticals. Jonathan was pushing for expansion and Alex had a quota looming over his head. Personally, he had wondered if SyncAnalytix would be more successful focusing on just the oil & gas market.

"Have you had a chance to follow-up on the two oil & gas leads from our last meeting?" Alex asked.

Mark was silent for a moment on the other end of the line. "It's been hit or miss, but mostly miss. I'll try calling them again this week in-between travel and meetings. Maybe I'll have something for you next week."

"Let's make it a priority," Alex said. "I don't want those leads to go cold."

"Will do. Listen, I have to sign off a little early to catch my flight to Sacramento. Any other questions before I go?" Mark asked.

"Or for me?" Maria piped up, "I've still got fifteen minutes before my next call."

To be honest, Alex was ready for this meeting to end. Maybe when he'd first sat down in the conference room, he had been expecting a breakthrough from one of them, instead he was hearing the same, lack of progress reports he'd been getting the last few weeks.

"No," he said, "Have a safe trip Mark, and we'll talk more about Dane Security when we have Jonathan on the line. Maria, I'll follow up with you later on Brexar."

"Sounds good!" she said.

All three of them left the call, and Alex leaned back in his chair in the empty conference room. Somehow, he was already dreading their next pipeline meeting. Lately too many meetings seemed to end with that sense that nothing had moved forward. He got up from the conference table and went back to his office.

3
MARKETING

Denise, the head of Marketing at SyncAnalytix, appeared to have a clear agenda when she walked into Jonathan's office for their 9:30 am meeting. Over the past few months, she'd been showing up to meetings like she just wanted to get them over with, more or less mirroring how Jonathan had been feeling about their marketing duties lately. But this time she had a determined look on her face and sat down in the chair in front of Jonathan's desk right away.

"I've got a lot of things to talk about today," she said. "I hope you're not about to tell me we need to reschedule because of an emergency developer meeting."

"Is it time for marketing again?" Jonathan asked without turning from his monitor, a hint of sarcasm in his voice. His tone got more serious when he said, "Alex is traveling, I figured we weren't going to meet without Alex."

Denise sat in silence and waited for Jonathan to give her his full attention. Finally, he caught on; he turned away from his computer, and Denise gave him a small, tight smile.

Jonathan rubbed his eyes, which were already sore after staring at the computer since he'd arrived at 7:30 am. "Okay, I guess we're meeting without Alex. What do you have on your agenda for us to talk about?"

Denise's expression softened a little. She immediately started speaking with more energy and gesturing with her hands.

"Well, for one, resources. Even though I appreciate the intern we were able to bring onboard—"

"Ethan?"

"Yes. He's a big help, but we're still grossly understaffed in Marketing," Denise pointed out, clearly frustrated. "There are a lot of things I want to be doing to support the Sales Team, but I don't have the bandwidth to do it all, even with an extra set of hands."

Jonathan tilted his head to the side, "Are there items in the marketing plan that are unfinished? I know some of the brochures still aren't ready for the European conference, but I'm confident you'll pull it together."

Denise let out a quiet sigh. She was trying not to take out her frustration on Jonathan, but it was hard when it always felt like she was making her requests to a brick wall. She tried again to make the situation clear, "I'm constantly getting requests for collateral from Sales, but what I really need to be working on is product marketing, to find and speak to our target customers. Without clarity on our target customers," she explained, "their use cases, and how SyncAnalytix solves their problems, our marketing material is just TechnoLatin that no one understands."

Jonathan thought this over for a moment. Or at least, it looked like he did.

"I think the brochures and other collateral you've been working on look great," he finally said. "Besides, our customers are highly technical, so they like all those technical terms that we use to describe our products."

"I don't think they do," Denise insisted. "Our bounce rates on the website are really high, and time spent on-site is low. I just don't think our message is resonating."

Jonathan's smartphone made that familiar pinging noise. Another chat notification. He instinctively turned back to his computer and started typing. "Hold that thought," he said, "I need to answer this question to keep the developers moving forward. We're trying to push through a new feature in order to close the FortenHurd deal."

"I'm concerned that we might be focusing on the wrong things," she pressed over the sound of Jonathan's typing.

Jonathan finished his response to the notification and turned back to Denise. "Wrong things?" he asked rhetorically. "Right now, the priority has to be scaling, so I think it makes sense that sales is where the focus goes."

Jonathan paused, remembering his recent lunch with Vaughn, "Do you think we should be focusing on something else?"

"There's marketing work that we need to do that should come before scaling, not come after," Denise said. "You can't make sales without good marketing."

"I disagree," Jonathan responded. "I managed to close two sales before SyncAnalytix even *had* a Marketing Department, remember?"

"Sure," Denise answered, clearly not wanting to get into another conversation where Jonathan indirectly communicated that he didn't consider her department to be a priority. Still, she'd come into this meeting with a goal. "I need at least one additional resource so we can better support all these requests that Alex and his team keep sending me. I even heard last week that we might be adding a perpetual license model and that there's a licensing agreement in the works with Dane Security. That's two new business models and another vertical where we have no marketing strategy in place."

"I don't know," Jonathan answered, "I don't think that's a good idea. We just don't have the budget. We need to hire an account executive for the southeast region if we want to have any chance of getting sales back on track to meet forecast."

Denise nodded once again. It was always the same story when she made a request for Marketing. Brick Wall 37, Marketing Department 0.

"In that case I better get back to work on the materials for Europe." Denise stood up to leave. "Anything else?"

"Nope," Jonathan answered, smiling. "Wait, did Alex talk to you about going to the tradeshow? He needs an extra hand manning the booth."

"He mentioned it, but I thought he was kidding," Denise responded. "I mean, where am I going to find time to go to Europe for a tradeshow?"

"Well, think about it and let me know," Jonathan added. He turned back to his computer screen. "And keep up the good work."

It doesn't feel like anything is working, Denise thought as she walked back to her cubicle.

4
CONVERSATIONAL IQ

Jonathan wasn't convinced that attending a talk on Conversational IQ was worth missing another evening at home, especially when evenings at home were something of a rarity, but Vaughn seemed more insistent than usual in recommending the event. Jonathan reached out to Vaughn's executive assistant, Hannah, to see if she had more details. She responded right away.

> V said something about an IQ meeting and a speaker named Helen, ring a bell?

> Do you mean Helen Pearson?
> She's doing a talk on C-IQ

> Yeah, that's probably it

> Tomorrow night at the new library
> Do you want me to register you?

> That would be great. Anything I should know about this special talk?

> It's casual, starts at 7pm
> Helen is really awesome!

Awesome? Jonathan thought, *she's doing a whole talk just about talking. How awesome could it be?*

It had been about two years since Jonathan had attended a networking event, and even longer since he'd been a speaker at one. When BlackBee was in a rapid growth phase, Jonathan had been invited to speak at a few events. Being in demand felt good. It had fed his ego quite a bit to get up and talk about the exciting new technology they had been developing.

The feel of this event was different. The crowd was a bit older, more diverse, and less technical than what Jonathan was used to.

He settled into the back row, looked around to see if there was anyone he recognized, and then looked down at his smartphone. He scrolled through his email hoping that his apathetic behavior would make it clear to those around him that he wasn't at this networking event to actually *network*.

A little after 7pm, the seats were filled up, and the conversations quieted down as someone stepped up to the podium. The emcee welcomed everyone to the event, made a few announcements, and then introduced the speaker: Helen Pearson. Jonathan was too busy typing on his phone to catch the content of her introduction. The crowd burst into laughter a moment later and he looked up, saw a new speaker on stage and thought, *ah, here's the famous Helen.* He put his smartphone in his pocket. *Let's see if she can tell me how to have an intelligent conversation about when to scale.*

Helen spent the next 30 minutes or so giving examples of different ways to create shared meaning within an organization and how to move to a place of co-creating. Jonathan was already familiar with some of the structures and guidelines she presented, but her references to emotional intelligence and its ties to Conversational Intelligence gave him a few "a-ha" moments when he thought about some recent meetings that hadn't gone so well. He made a mental note to apply some of what he heard. Helen was a polished speaker; she wrapped up her talk just before Jonathan reached the edge of thinking, *this is too much to remember.* She opened up the floor to questions.

"Something you mentioned earlier in your talk struck me. Do people really form impressions that easily before they've even gotten to know each other?" a man on the second row asked.

"We can feel if someone is judging us, even if they haven't said a word to us yet," Helen began. "And, of course, it works the same way if someone is accepting us."

"From their body language?" someone piped up from a few rows back.

"Something like that," Helen continued, and if she was bothered by the interruption, it didn't show. "It comes out in all of the small details of the way you give someone your attention, even before the conversation begins. There's research to support that these first, unspoken connections are the deciding factor in how easily we open up to one another and how much we share with them."

Someone else raised the question, "What if you instinctively don't like someone? Can you still pull off the whole 'I accept you' routine to get them to feel comfortable?"

The question made Helen smile, and the audience laughed a little bit. Jonathan saw some people still taking down notes from Helen's last answer. He wondered if he should have written some of this down. With everything going on back at work, there was a good chance it'd leave his mind as soon as he stepped back into the office.

"Even if you started off on the wrong foot, there are things you can do to address biases, barriers, and blind spots that could be the source of disconnect.

"The most important thing is to be transparent and curious," was Helen's final answer.

A few more questions were asked, all of them getting a response that was somehow highly professional and relatable at the same time. As the crowd got quiet and the program wrapped up, the emcee came back up to the podium. He thanked Helen for her thoughts, invited everyone to stay afterwards to network, and then led a round of applause.

Jonathan lingered in his seat for a few minutes while the rest of the audience headed towards the open hallway to socialize. A line of people waiting to meet Helen started to form near the podium. Jonathan was intrigued himself, not just because of Vaughn's insistence that he should meet her, but because of her presentation, as well. As he drew closer, he could tell that many of them were lining up to ask questions they'd been too uncomfortable to ask in front of the whole group. Some whispered, stuttered, or even blushed when they made it to the front of the line, and one woman even teared up as Helen embraced her and spoke quietly in her ear. At first Jonathan thought about just following up with her later using the contact information she'd shared, but the long line moved quickly as Helen skillfully addressed each person waiting for her attention.

By the time Jonathan got to the front of the line he had decided on which compliment he would use before introducing himself.

"I liked what you said about breaking the ice with relational talk at the start of the meeting. I sort of struggle with that, myself. I tend to want to get right to the point and discuss specifics; but now I'm thinking that it probably gives the impression that I don't care." Jonathan had no idea how he ended up rambling when he was only going to offer a short compliment, but Helen was listening attentively the entire time. He cleared his throat and held out his hand to introduce himself. "I'm Jonathan Reeves."

"Hi Jonathan," Helen responded with a smile. "Hannah mentioned that you might be here."

"Oh, how do you know Hannah?" Jonathan asked.

"I've done a few projects with Vaughn and met Hannah in the process."

"Speaking of Vaughn, I'm here because he said I should meet you," Jonathan said, "Although I'm not sure why he was so insistent. No offense. It's just that I'm having an issue with one of my VPs, and I don't see how Conversational IQ ties into it."

Jonathan realized he'd just given too much information again, but he couldn't find it in him to feel awkward about it the second time. He was starting to suspect that Helen simply had this effect on people, which meant she was probably used to it by now.

"Conversational IQ impacts team dynamics, maybe that's what Vaughn was thinking," Helen said. "I'd be happy to meet and discuss this in more detail. I'm glad we had a chance to connect."

Before Jonathan could respond, Helen had already finished shaking his hand and had moved her attention to the person waiting behind him. Jonathan wasn't sure if he should get back in line to attempt another question, even though he felt tempted to do so. Then again, he'd accomplished what Vaughn had told him to do: he had met Helen. He decided to slip out of the crowd and into the hallway, weaving through groups of networkers.

On his way to the exit, Jonathan paused when he noticed Amir on the edge of the crowd, talking to a small group of three.

He and Amir had both been entrepreneurs-in-residence at Meranti Ventures after Jonathan exited BlackBee and started his transition into the venture side of tech startups. They had worked together on evaluating opportunities until Amir left to lead a rollup, and Jonathan left soon after and founded SyncAnalytix. They had lost touch after going their separate ways, so Jonathan happily took a detour to join Amir's group.

"Room for one more?" he asked.

Amir lit up when Jonathan entered the group and stopped mid-sentence, "I thought that was you! I wasn't sure at first since it's been, what, two years already?" he boomed. "What have you been up to, Jon, how are you? Have you lost weight? You look great."

Jonathan was pleased to see that his friend hadn't changed at all in those two years. "It's great to see you," he replied. "And great to get some compliments."

"Anytime! I just can't believe we ran into each other here, of all places! You've got your hands full with SyncAnalytix, I heard."

Jonathan knew that was another compliment, but he could only think of what he actually had his hands full with at SyncAnalytix: a sales issue which was turning into a staff issue which was turning into a management issue. Still, he tried to look appreciative, especially in front of the rest of the group.

"Well, anyway, I didn't mean to interrupt. I just wanted to say 'hi.' I was just about to head back to the office."

"Still burning the candle at both ends! Some things never change, folks," Amir said to the rest of the group. "I have to head out as well, you know. But not back to the office in case you're all wondering." He turned back to Jonathan, "Mind if I join you on your way out?"

Jonathan figured *why not* and nodded. Amir said his goodbyes, and they both made their way towards the parking garage.

"I was surprised to see you at the meeting tonight," Amir said, with less energy and less volume now that they'd left the group setting. "I always thought you were great at communicating strategy. What's left for you to learn?"

"I like to think so," Jonathan said with a smile. "I guess some people still think I'm lacking in the 'emotional intelligence' part, though. Vaughn told me I needed to meet Helen."

"If Vaughn told you to meet Helen, it probably wasn't for Conversational IQ," Amir replied. "She's an executive coach, you know, and a very good one, but you heard all that in the intro." Amir paused when he saw the blank look on Jonathan's face. "...So, how are things at SyncAnalytix? Did Vaughn want Helen to help you with something?"

"They could always be better," Jonathan sighed a little. "Feels like there's always more work to be done. But isn't that what running a startup is all about?"

Amir raised his eyebrows and shrugged his shoulders.

Jonathan felt like they were at Meranti Ventures all over again, learning through trial and error and a good deal of guessing. But he was interrupted in his memories when he realized something. He stopped in his tracks in the half-lit garage and turned to Amir, "Do you think Vaughn wants me to hire an executive coach?"

Amir stared back at him. "You don't already have one? Getting a coach was one of the best things I did when I left Meranti. It completely stepped up my game. Took me to the next level."

"Oh, really?" Jonathan asked. He wasn't sure if he believed that an executive coach was all it took.

"I'm not kidding. The right executive coach will help you find the solution to your problem which could be hidden in your subconscious the whole time. It's also about those things that you can't discuss with the board, and can't tell your employees, and if you tell your wife, it could strain your marriage."

Jonathan let out a chuckle. He definitely had *some* things like that. Things he'd figured just needed to stay bottled up until they somehow got solved. He had no idea there was another option.

"Wait, is Helen your coach?" he asked.

"No, but I've heard really great things about her. Unfortunately, she wasn't in coaching yet when I started Fast Growth Capital. Wish she was. You know what? You should follow up with her, see if you can get a meeting."

"I'll think about it, but I don't know if I really need a coach. I just have one specific issue with one of my executives. Everything else I can handle on my own."

"Some people say executive transition is one of those things you *need* to get a coach for," Amir shrugged. "If Vaughn recommended her, it must be because he thinks she'll help."

"Maybe I'll call her. At the very least to figure out what the big deal is. I feel like I'm out of some sort of loop. I'm starting to wonder if my title isn't actually 'CEO,' but 'CEO in Training' and nobody told me," Jonathan joked.

"Aw, come on, don't say that!" Amir pressed the button on his key fob a couple times until his car lit up. "You've come so far since BlackBee. And this Series A thing? Incredible. In fact, I'll probably be reading about a Series B in the near future—especially if there's any truth to that 'joint venture with Halskee' rumor."

Jonathan reached out to shake Amir's hand. "It was great running into you tonight. We should get coffee or lunch soon and catch up."

"Yeah, we've got *lots* to talk about."

Jonathan raised an eyebrow at him.

"Halskee?" Amir inquired again.

Jonathan rolled his eyes and headed to his own car. "No comment," he replied over his shoulder with a smile.

As Jonathan drove out of the garage he reflected on his conversation with Amir:

If Vaughn thinks I should meet with Helen, and Amir thinks I should meet with Helen, I guess I should meet with Helen.

5
SALES STRATEGY

Jonathan was intrigued by what he'd heard about Helen Pearson. From what Vaughn said about her, he'd hoped seeing her presentation would clear some things up for him, but he wasn't quite so lucky. At the C-IQ event, the talk itself hardly seemed relevant to his situation, and he didn't really get a chance to gauge whether or not she'd be able to help him with his sales issue when they talked one-on-one. He almost felt like she'd brushed him off amidst the long line of people waiting to talk to her. Still, his conversation with Amir on his way out left him with a nagging feeling that he should try to meet with her to see if coaching might help.

He reached out via email about a follow-up meeting and was surprised that someone who seemed so in demand was able to pencil him in a week later.

At her—somewhat subtle—insistence, they met at Helen's office instead of at SyncAnalytix. Jonathan would have liked to save time by having her come to his office and pulling away from his work was even more difficult when the day came, but he made it there on time. Almost.

"Sorry I'm late," he said as her assistant showed him into the conference room where Helen had been waiting. She stood up when he arrived, and they shook hands before returning to the table.

"Did you have trouble finding us?" Helen asked.

"No, I just got held up at the office on a software issue. I didn't want my team to be stuck while I was away for this meeting."

Helen nodded.

"Before we get started, I like to ask, have you ever worked with a coach before?" Helen began. The question surprised Jonathan. He had expected—hoped, to be honest—that they would get right to work.

"An executive coach? No, the last time I had a coach was in high school track," Jonathan joked.

"What was that experience like for you?"

"Well, he was called a coach, but everyone thought he was more of a dictator. He was the varsity football coach, and I think they gave him track in the spring so he would have something to do." Jonathan leaned back in his chair and wondered if there was anything else he needed to add. The conversation already seemed to be going wildly off topic.

"Everyone thought he was a dictator," Helen reflected. "Why do you think they thought that?"

"Probably because he was always telling us what to do. He had everything planned for us." Jonathan lifted up both hands in surrender. "You know, he 'coached' us."

"That sounds like what a high school coach would be responsible for," Helen added. "Can you think of anything specific that would cause him to be labeled a dictator?"

"Oh yeah," Jonathan smiled. "He called himself that."

"Interesting, tell me more about that."

"Well, it was the week before district competitions, and our top pole vaulter didn't want to compete in the meet because she thought she should save her energy for districts. Well, Coach wasn't going to have that, so he pulled the team together and made it clear that he was the coach, and he would decide when we would compete and when we would save our energy. Then, and I remember this like it was yesterday, he said, 'This is not a republic. You do not get to vote on what you are going to do. This is a dictatorship, and I'm in charge.'"

Helen took a deep breath and made a few notes on her notepad. It was more of a cleansing breath, but Jonathan noticed and wondered if he had said something wrong.

"Probably not the coaching experience you were expecting to hear about," Jonathan added.

"I appreciate you sharing that," Helen said. "I have a feeling it will frame your response to my next question, but I will ask it anyway. What expectations do you have for me as a coach?"

"Well, I don't expect you to give me the dictator speech," Jonathan laughed. Helen smiled in return but maintained focus which encouraged Jonathan to continue. "I do actually hope you'll tell me what to do, though, and answer some questions that Vaughn raised in our last meeting—since you seem to know him pretty well."

Helen paused before answering.

"You will find that executive coaching is a very different experience," Helen began. "You might be a little disappointed to learn that I won't be telling you what to do or answering questions you have about what someone else is thinking. Actually, quite the opposite."

Jonathan could tell from her practiced response that she probably had to make clarifications like this all the time.

"How helpful can coaching be if you don't tell me what to do or answer my questions?"

"In my experience, clients usually know what to do. They know the answers, or they know someone on their team who can help them get to the answers."

Helen paused again to see if Jonathan had anything further to add. Sensing he did not, she continued.

"What we're going to do today is an introductory coaching session. Depending on how things go, and what you get from the conversation, you can decide if this is something that you find valuable and wish to continue."

Jonathan resisted the urge to ask how *valuable* might translate to *cost* because he was eager to get started, and eager to get back to work. He wasn't much for small talk even when he didn't have an agenda, and now more than ever he had been hoping they could jump straight to the point.

Instead, they'd just spent a good chunk of their scheduled time talking about something completely unrelated to SyncAnalytix. Jonathan tried his best not to consider it time wasted.

"If you don't have any more questions, we can get started by me asking you the first question: what is the most important thing for us to talk about today?"

"I'm going to assume that you haven't actually talked to Vaughn about what's going on," Jonathan began. "Is that a good assumption?"

"That's correct. Vaughn and I haven't spoken about you, and anything we discuss here today is confidential."

"Well, that's probably a good policy," Jonathan said, even though he felt a little disappointed that Vaughn hadn't talked to Helen at all about what was going on. As embarrassing as it might have felt if Helen answered differently, at least it would've sped things up today.

"So, to answer your original question, two things come to mind. But probably the most important thing is whether or not I should fire my VP of Sales."

"What is the other thing that came to mind," Helen asked, adding, "just in case the two are related."

"When is the right time to scale?" And then Jonathan added, "but that falls under a whole different issue of 'trying to understand Vaughn,' and it seems like you won't be helping me with that."

Helen listened closely while Jonathan spoke, resting her chin on her hand. It was a little bit strange, compared to their first interaction, to have her patient and undivided attention. Finally, she nodded and asked:

"What do you mean by 'when is the right time to scale?'"

"I have no idea," Jonathan said, and he must have sounded as frustrated as he felt. "I thought you would know since Vaughn asked me that question after I asked if I should fire my VP of Sales."

"Ok, so if I'm hearing you correctly, you had a conversation with Vaughn about whether you should fire your VP of Sales, and he asked you if it was the right time to scale."

"Yeah, exactly. And then he said something about customer discovery."

"And what does customer discovery mean?" Helen asked.

"I don't know, but I have a sinking feeling I should know that. I was going to do some research, but I've been really busy working on a new product release. Couldn't find the time."

"Fire the VP, right time to scale, and customers. Those sound like common CEO dilemmas," Helen began. "What sort of outcome from our discussion of these questions would make this time feel worth it to you?"

"Honestly, I was hoping you could just give me some answers to them, but that's not how this works, is it?"

Helen shook her head no.

"So, then I guess if I had a plan for how to get those answers, it would be worth it."

"Who could help you find out?" Helen asked.

"Vaughn said customer discovery had something to do with marketing. If I follow that line of thought, then the plan would be to ask my Marketing Team."

It seemed easy once Jonathan said it out loud. He could bring it up in the next meeting with Denise, and it probably would take significantly less time than if Jonathan tried to research the issue on his own.

Helen waited for Jonathan to finish thinking about that before continuing. "What about 'right time to scale,'" she asked next, "what thoughts do you have about that question?"

"I've been thinking about it a lot, and I'm starting to think Vaughn meant it as a strategy question—meaning, should the company be focusing on scaling, or something else?"

"What might the 'something else' be?"

Jonathan thought for a moment, then decided to turn the tables a bit. Even if she wouldn't tell him exactly what he was supposed to do, he was sure that she had to have some sort of opinion on this.

"I'm at a loss here. What do you think 'something else' could be? I'm sure you've had other clients that experienced this problem. What did they do?"

Helen smiled. "They usually work out these issues as a leadership team. Have you talked to your team about your conversation with Vaughn and the questions he posed?"

"No, no, no," Jonathan said, waving his hands. "I can't share that conversation with them, especially considering that part of the conversation was about whether or not to fire one of them."

"Taking the termination question out," Helen said, "What do you think your team would have to say about the sales strategy and customer discovery?"

"That, like me, they are too busy to get into management theories, and we just need to execute."

"So, that tells me that the sales strategy is correct, and what you are doing in customer discovery is on track, you just need to hire more resources?" Helen asked. "Is that what you mean when you say everyone just needs to execute?"

Jonathan dragged a hand down his face. He felt like he'd just backed himself into a corner.

"Is this relevant? I feel like we're getting further from the issue of whether or not I should fire my VP of Sales."

"Okay," Helen said. She allowed the conversation to pivot, seemingly unfazed by Jonathan's accusatory tone. "Let's zero in on that. Why do you feel like you need to fire your VP of Sales?"

"Because he's missed quota two quarters in a row."

"And how do you attribute that to your VP of Sales?" Helen asked.

"I'm not sure what you're asking," Jonathan replied. "The VP of Sales is responsible for the quota, so if he's missing it, then I need to make a change. I mean, that's what the CEO needs to do. Ultimately, *I'm* responsible for the performance of my team, and the board knows that."

"Ok, let me ask it a different way, what other factors could be causing the Sales Team to miss quota?"

"Execution, I guess. Things like how many calls they're making, how many customer meetings, how 'good' they are at sales, basically." Jonathan responded.

"Anything else?"

Jonathan paused. He wasn't sure what he'd been expecting from a conversation with an executive coach, and he had been told already not to expect advice on what to do, but it still felt like she was interrogating him more than anything. He couldn't imagine that this was what true coaching was, compared to the anecdote he had shared from high school. Even if coaches weren't supposed to be dictators, they were supposed to *help* the process somehow, he was convinced, not just observe it.

The questions she was asking didn't seem to actually be highlighting the issue, either, or presenting a solution. Mostly Jonathan was starting to feel defensive. He tried not to show it.

"Well, anything else would be outside their control," Jonathan began.

"Like what?"

"The product, the marketing, the strategy." Jonathan paused and looked at Helen with a blank stare. He then tilted his head slightly to the right and said, "What we should be selling and who we should be selling to. That *is* something we could control, but it is outside of the Sales Team. I guess if I took it to the extreme then it could mean the sales strategy is wrong."

"Tell me more about that," Helen encouraged Jonathan to continue. "How would you know if the sales strategy was wrong?"

Jonathan let out a deep sigh. "It would be wrong if the reason we aren't making sales turned out to be that nobody was clear on the target market and customers. If we were trying to sell to anyone we could."

Helen nodded. "Can you tell me more about that, being clear on the target market and customers?"

"I thought we were being opportunistic going after new markets. Now that I think about it, it feels like we are hoping for the best instead of having a clear strategy on what market we should be in and going after that market."

"With that in mind, do you need to fire your VP of Sales or is there a different solution?" she asked.

Jonathan didn't understand how she could ask a question like that as if he knew the answer. If he knew what a different solution was instead of firing Alex, he wouldn't have come to this meeting. He tried to think of a response that would at least seem like he was trying to answer her question, and what came out was:

"If the solution isn't firing Alex, then we need to fix the sales strategy. Because if the team isn't the problem, then the strategy must be wrong."

And there it was. Jonathan was so bothered that he didn't just come up with that on his own that he almost missed the question Helen asked next.

"Are you willing to address that between now and our next session?" Helen asked.

Jonathan shifted uneasily in his chair.

Not sure where Jonathan's reluctance was coming from, Helen asked, "What are you avoiding?"

"One, I'm not sure where to begin," Jonathan responded, "and two, we should know this already. We launched our product almost a year ago. Am *I* the problem if I say we don't have a working strategy?"

"It sounds like it would be a challenge for you to say the sales strategy is not working."

"What about the fact that I'm not sure how I'd even start that conversation?"

"That would be challenging to come to terms with for any CEO. Have you met with your team to discuss your sales strategy before?"

"Now that I think about it, no," Jonathan answered, clearly discouraged. "We decided on a quota before we hired most of them," he added, hoping Helen didn't ask who 'we' referred to. "The focus has been on hitting quota."

"How do you think your team would respond if you engaged them in a strategy discussion?"

The question caught Jonathan off guard, but what surprised him even more was the fact that he didn't know how to answer it at first. He tried to think back to his most recent meetings with Alex and Denise and his memory came up disappointingly short. He didn't know how either of them would handle talking about strategy; maybe they never had.

"I honestly have no idea.," he admitted.

"Is it worth a try?"

Jonathan sighed. "It can't make things any worse, can it?"

"So, even with all the unknowns, is having a strategy discussion with your team something you would be willing to commit to?"

Once again, Jonathan didn't feel satisfied with any of the ways he could think of to answer that question. He knew he was supposed to just say yes, but it wasn't that simple.

"We still haven't addressed the fact that I don't even know where to begin."

"Can I offer a suggestion?" Helen asked.

Jonathan nodded 'yes.' *Now we're getting somewhere,* he thought.

"You can start by being open to a discussion and then see where that goes. I think you know more about where to begin than you give yourself credit for," Helen said. It was the first time she'd said something that felt like it earned the term 'coaching.'

"Yes, I can have a discussion with the team," Jonathan decided, and realized a little too late that Helen was going to hold him to that commitment. "I'm not sure where it will lead, but I can give it a try."

Helen smiled as she put her notepad down on the table and pulled out a document.

Sensing that the conversation was wrapping up, Jonathan noticed the time and immediately felt anxious about being disconnected from his phone for the past forty-five minutes.

"Before you head out, I wanted to get your thoughts on today's conversation. Do you feel we addressed your most important topic?" Helen asked.

"Yes, thank you," Jonathan answered.

He heard himself stumbling over his response a little, even now when they'd moved from talking about the company to talking about the conversation they'd had about the company. "I couldn't see where things were going, but that's probably because I had my head up my ass. So, I won't fire our VP of Sales yet," Jonathan said with a wry smile.

"Great," Helen said. "If you decide you want to continue with coaching, here is my standard coaching agreement." Helen handed Jonathan the document she had pulled from her notebook. "I encourage my clients to look at it and make it more tailored to their specific needs, but I'll let you do that on your own time since our conversation today was more urgent for you. I'm glad you were able to work through some questions, and I look forward to hearing how your strategy discussions go with your team."

"Thank you, again," Jonathan said as he got up from his chair. "This discussion *has* been helpful. Even though I was hoping for you to just give me some answers, I actually feel a little less stuck than when I first got here."

He had planned on taking more time to consider whether he wanted to bother with hiring an executive coach, but even after the discomfort he'd been through in the last hour, he couldn't deny that he'd had more solid realizations about his sales issue than in the past six months of team and board meetings combined.

Helen got up to see Jonathan to the door. "Marsha can validate your parking and coordinate schedules if you would like to meet again. I would recommend meeting once a week. Until then, I wish you the best in working through your sales strategy!"

Jonathan nodded as he walked out of the conference room. He felt exhausted, and he had only been *talking* about what was going on at SyncAnalytix, he wasn't actually sitting in front of his computer *working*. It was no wonder everyone seemed to be stretched thin right now.

6
CUSTOMER DISCOVERY

Jonathan made it back to his office just in time to hop on the weekly pipeline sales call. He dialed into the bridge and introduced himself before putting his phone on mute.

He had taken a break from the weekly calls for the past couple of months but decided to re-engage after last quarter's forecast was missed by such a large margin. While he listened passively to the Sales Team report on last week's meetings and this week's plan, he sent a message to Denise, to see if she could pull her team together for a quick meeting in 20 minutes.

Jonathan continued to multi-task. He listened to Alex ask questions of the Sales Team while answering emails and the occasional chat message. He finally refocused on the sales call when he heard someone mention a competitive bid situation with OscarIoT. He took his phone off mute.

"What do you think our chances are against OscarIoT?" Jonathan asked. "Do they have something new that's going to pull customers away from our software?"

Mark responded, "It shouldn't be a problem, I don't think. The buyer owes me a favor, so if we have to lower our price, he'll give me a heads-up. I doubt that OscarIoT will even bid for the deal."

Something about the answer didn't sit right with Jonathan. First and foremost, it wasn't much of an answer at all. Maybe his tendency to be dismissive of his employees' anxiety had become contagious. He let it slide, though, and decided to bring it up later with Alex directly. As the call was finishing up, Denise and her team appeared in front of Jonathan's office.

Well, 'team' was probably too generous.

Denise and her intern, Ethan, waited patiently at the door while Jonathan said his goodbyes to the Sales Team and signed off from the call.

He invited them both inside and closed the door as they sat down in front of his desk.

"So how is the Marketing Department today?" Jonathan asked with a hint of sarcasm.

"We're great," Denise answered, "how's the Sales Team doing?"

"They're trying," he responded. He turned off his computer screen so he could focus on the conversation at hand. "Anyway, I've been thinking about our sales and marketing strategy at SyncAnalytix, and I'm wondering if you can help me understand what our marketing approach has been so far."

"Oh. That's a pretty big question. I'm not sure if I know where to start." Denise laughed a little bit, shifted in her chair and leaned forward. Her demeanor seemed different today, maybe because Jonathan was showing more interest in her work than he usually did. Their last few meetings had mostly been for the purpose of Denise giving updates and Jonathan giving a thumbs up.

Or, maybe more often than either of them would like, a thumbs down.

"Could you be a bit more specific?" Denise asked.

"Maybe it would help if I started by describing what I think Marketing should be doing," Jonathan began.

He had been thinking over how he would word that suggestion since his meeting with Helen. It sounded odd even to his own ears, but he tried to remember what he'd finally told her when she asked if he would be willing to initiate strategy discussions with his team— that it can't make things any worse.

Denise's posture stiffened right away. Jonathan caught the way Ethan's eyes widened and his eyebrows drew together in confusion before he tried to play it cool. He could feel their discomfort and offered, "I don't think you're doing anything wrong; I just thought it might be helpful to start there."

"Ok," Denise responded, still a bit tense. "What do you think Marketing should be doing?"

Jonathan felt a bit unsure, even though he'd put himself on the spot willingly. He powered through. "So, my perspective is that Marketing's job is to communicate our product to our customers and highlight what makes us different from the competition. Maybe that seems kind of obvious, but does that at least make sense?"

Denise took a moment to gather her thoughts.

"Yes, that makes sense. We do have a lot of different initiatives going on in marketing, mainly the website, blog, social media, PR, and tradeshows. All of those are created to help build awareness of our products and the company in general. But awareness and preference are only the first two steps to customer acquisition."

"Is customer acquisition the same as customer discovery?" Jonathan asked.

Denise looked over to Ethan. "Customer discovery is lean startup stuff," she responded. "That's why Ethan is here."

"Really?" Jonathan asked as he moved his focus from Denise to Ethan. "You mean he's not here to make copies?"

His joke didn't exactly land. Ethan offered a weak sort of smile.

"He's not that kind of intern," Denise continued, "he's here working on his capstone project."

"Yeah. Uh, yes sir," Ethan said as he cautiously entered the conversation. "I'm—well, I'm researching lean startup to see how it applies to startups like SyncAnalytix."

"So where are you in the process?" Jonathan asked.

"Well, you know, I'm really not an expert on it. I only just read a lean startup book for my entrepreneurship class last semester. This is the part where I'm supposed to learn how it all works," Ethan said, before quickly adding,

"According to my professors. I mean, that's what they said."

"Lean startup is primarily about transforming how new products are built and launched," Denise offered. "Ethan has only been here for two weeks, and with everything going on, we haven't had much time to focus on his project, yet."

"Fair enough, I didn't mean to put you on the spot," Jonathan said. "But can you tell me what customer discovery is and, well, honestly—if we're actually doing it?"

Ethan breathed out a laugh. Jonathan couldn't tell if it was nerves or discomfort.

"Well, I mean," Ethan started, "I can try. You probably know all this but basically customer discovery is like, step one in the customer development process. You're trying to figure out if your customers actually need what you think they need to solve their problem and then you can create an MVP to see if you're right. If you *are* right, you can do step two which is customer validation."

Jonathan was sure he must have been in one of the interviews while they were recruiting Ethan, but he couldn't remember if he'd ever heard the kid say so many words.

"Ok, that answers both my questions. And it's good to hear. Since we have an MVP then we must be done with customer discovery."

Ethan opened his mouth to respond to that and then seemed to change his mind.

"No, go ahead," Jonathan urged.

"Well, it's just that…I don't think it's actually that simple," Ethan offered up cautiously. "Again, I haven't been able to really spend time on this, but it looks like SyncAnalytix is trying to follow a more traditional new-product introduction process. So, the MVP is more like the beta version of the product. Just, uh, with a different name."

Jonathan didn't miss the implications in his language, even with how lightly Ethan was trying to tread on this topic. *Trying to* follow the traditional product introduction model, as opposed to actually following it.

"If I'm being honest, Ethan, that doesn't make sense to me," Jonathan responded. He didn't want to sound frustrated, but some of it might have been showing. Still, he was careful when he asked, "What makes you think that's what's going on?"

Ethan shifted uncomfortably in his chair. "Well, you know, the MVP is supposed to test assumptions about the ideal customer." Ethan paused as he looked over to Denise for assurance that he should continue—which she provided by nodding her head slightly.

"And, um. I haven't been able to find any material here on the ideal customer, or a problem definition or anything, so I just assumed that you weren't following the customer development process."

"Okay," Jonathan said, and wasn't sure how to address that. In the end he decided to follow his instincts. "This may come across as arrogant, but because I'm so deep in the technology, I tend to know more about what the customer needs than they do. Which is why as soon as we launched the product, I was able to quickly close the first two sales."

Sensing the tension in the room, Denise reengaged in the conversation to avoid overloading her intern's first extended interaction with the CEO.

"Well, technology aside, I read an HBR article about lean startup and I agree with Ethan. I think our approach is more aligned with the traditional model."

"Is that a problem?" Jonathan asked.

"It could be," Ethan proposed tentatively but paused to see if Denise would finish the thought.

"Right," Denise continued, "it could be a problem if we're wrong."

Now Jonathan was the one who paused to gather his thoughts. Whenever he showed the product to customers, he always received positive feedback. *How could he be wrong?*

"I don't think I know what you mean by wrong," Jonathan finally admitted. That word Helen had used when they talked about team meetings, *challenging*, only felt like half of what he was experiencing right now. He had unknowingly called the Marketing Team into his office just to reveal to them how little he knew, and he was supposed to be the one in charge.

Just as Jonathan finished that sentence, his desk phone rang. "Oh, shoot," he said, "this might be my 3:30 meeting. Hold that thought."

Jonathan spoke quickly to the person on the other end of the line. He apologized for running late and asked for five minutes to finish up another meeting. As he hung up the phone, he asked Denise and Ethan to walk with him to the Cognito conference room.

"Ethan," Jonathan turned to their intern, who had definitely stepped back into his comfort zone somewhere between Jonathan's office and the door of the conference room, only to be pulled out again by his next question, "Do you think you can pull together a presentation on the lean startup concepts you find relevant and present something to me and Alex on Friday?"

"Do you mean, um, 'tomorrow' Friday, or 'next week' Friday?" Ethan asked, his concern clear in his facial expression.

"I guess tomorrow," Jonathan responded. "Welcome to the world of startups. Denise, can you confirm with Alex that 3:30 tomorrow works on his calendar. Oh, and Ethan," he said as he opened the door to the conference room, "just put together some basic stuff, don't worry about making a big presentation. I don't want to dig too deep, but I think we need to start looking at this sooner rather than later, especially the idea that we could be getting it 'wrong.' And I want Alex and Denise's thoughts on this ASAP."

"Okay," Ethan nodded. He looked just as afraid as before.

"That's probably too aggressive a schedule," Denise interrupted. "Can we make it Monday, so Ethan and I have enough time to prepare? I might also have thoughts on where we stand with customer discovery."

She had a point. Jonathan didn't know if Ethan was going to be able to pull it together in one day. On top of that, Denise seemed more engaged by the end of their meeting than she had been in the past few months. He was interested to see what she would have to contribute to the conversation as well.

"Ok," Jonathan responded as he entered the conference room. "If Monday afternoon works for Alex, let's do it then."

Jonathan sat down for his next meeting with just a hint of a feeling that their meeting had made a difference just now. Before turning to focus on the product backlog and story points on the screen, he stopped at the realization—*did Denise say she has thoughts about customer discovery? And she's just now bringing it up?*

7
LEAN STARTUP

Ethan walked into the conference room on Monday looking like a zombie. He had definitely pulled an all-nighter or two in preparation for their meeting.

He is a college student after all, Jonathan thought, *he can handle a sleepless night every now and then.*

Alex and Denise followed soon after. As Alex sat down, he asked Jonathan if he should conference in the Sales Team.

Jonathan shook his head, "No, not this time. This is a high-level meeting, and I don't want to distract your team from making sales calls right now."

"That's good," Alex replied. "They're busy working on a counter to the OscarIoT bid on Dane Security."

Jonathan's eyes widened in concern.

"OscarIoT *actually* submitted a bid to Dane Security? I thought they were supposed to pass."

Alex sighed. "They submitted a pretty competitive bid. They didn't even know we were looking to partner with Dane Security until the Dane CFO called them. We're not a perfect fit, so I think we'll really need to trim our margins."

"Damn," Jonathan muttered. "I was counting on that agreement to pull us out of our slump."

"It still can," Alex replied reassuringly. "We just need to get past this slight hiccup. Mark has a good relationship with the sponsor, so he should tell us exactly how to win the deal. I just wanted to give you a heads-up that it might require an exclusive commitment or a bigger discount."

"Whatever it takes," Jonathan said. "Keep me in the loop, I don't want to lose any business to OscarIoT if we can help it."

Denise had been listening intently to the news about Dane Security, sitting next to Ethan who looked more or less awake. As soon as she seemed to sense a break in the conversation, she interjected.

"We should start the meeting before Ethan passes out. I'm worried there's only so much caffeine left in his system."

"There's still half a pot of coffee in the breakroom if you think he needs some more," Jonathan offered with a hint of a smile.

Denise gave him a flat look.

"Alright, alright. Let's get things moving," Jonathan finally said. "Ethan, you have the floor. Tell us all you've got about lean startup. I'm especially curious to know where we stand based on what you found out."

Alex nodded at that, too. "Feels like I'm back in college this afternoon," he said with a smile. "Just without the bad haircut."

Ethan was too busy gearing himself up to speak to respond to Alex's joke. He stood at the front of the conference room, now, looking a little uneasy.

"Ok, uh," he started. "So, I didn't have a lot of time because the more research I did, I sorta realized how much there is to the concept. Really there was too much to cover in one meeting, but I put together a few slides that we can talk through. And Denise and I came up with a couple areas where there might be room for improvement—I mean, if you wanted to implement any of this. We can start by talking about where Lean Startup concepts came from, I guess?"

"Is the history really important?" Jonathan asked as Ethan put up his first slide.

Lean Startup History

- *The Four Steps to the Epiphany: Successful Strategies for Products that Win*
  by Steve Blank, self-published 2005
- *Running Lean: Iterate from Plan A to a Plan That Works*
  by Ash Maurya, published 2010
- *The Lean Startup: How Today's Entrepreneurs Use Continuous Innovation to Create Radically Successful Businesses*
  by Eric Ries, published 2011
- *The Startup Owner's Manual: The Step-By-Step Guide for Building a Great Company*
  by Steve Blank and Bob Dorf, published 2012

1

"Wow, this thing has been around since 2005?" Alex asked, and Ethan, sleep deprived as he was, seemed to perk up a little bit. "I remember picking that book up around 2015, but I had no idea I was 10 years behind."

"Well, the book called *The Lean Startup®* is from 2011, but some of the initial concepts were actually published in Steve Blank's *The Four Steps to the Epiphany* which was in 2005."

Ethan paused to see if he should remain on the history slide or skip to the next one. The slide was really just a list of book titles.

Jonathan looked at Denise and asked, "have you read either of these books?"

"I've read parts of *The Lean Startup*," Denise replied, "but it's not exactly a how-to book."

"Right," Ethan continued. "It's pretty easy to read, though. Probably why it's so popular."

"And it's got a great title," Jonathan added.

Denise noticed that Jonathan seemed to be losing interest in the history lesson, so she asked Ethan to move on. "Are we ready to go to the next slide?"

"Yeah sure, sorry," Ethan verbally stumbled as he moved to the next slide. "So, customer development contains four different processes: customer discovery, customer validation, customer creation, and company building."

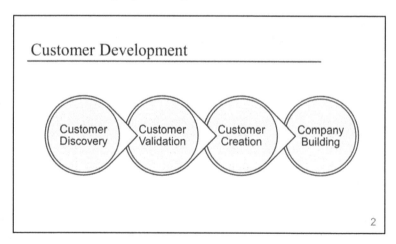

Now we're getting somewhere, Jonathan thought.

Ethan clicked to the next slide.

Customer Discovery

Translate company ideas into business model hypotheses

Test assumptions about customers' needs

Create a minimum viable product (MVP) to test solution

3

"Well, that seems pretty simple," Jonathan began, "and like stuff we're already doing. Right?"

His relief only lasted a few moments before the rest of his team responded to his question.

"I guess it must have been before my time," Alex shrugged.

"Well, parts of it," Denise interjected. "This description is pretty broad. We'll get into more of what these terms mean."

Ethan moved the presentation forward.

Business Model Hypotheses

* Market Size
* Product
* Customer & Problem
* Channel & Pricing
* Demand Creation
* Market Type
* Competitive

4

"I actually made this list from the books I mentioned," Ethan added. Everyone took a moment to read through the list.

"So, are these the company ideas, or the 'hypotheses', or what?" Jonathan asked.

"They're all different hypotheses. I have a slide for each one," Ethan responded.

He moved forward to the 'market' slide. On the screen was a grouping of concentric circles with the acronyms TAM and SAM, and a small circle in the middle labeled SOM.

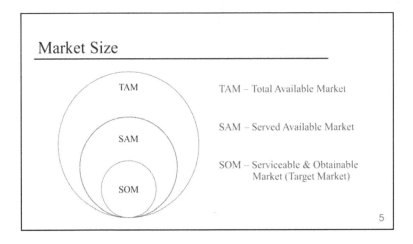

"The reason that market size is usually first on the list is because they say, 'there's nothing worse than spending years going after a small market'." Ethan looked over to Denise to see if she had anything else to add. She nodded.

"We've looked at the total market, and it's pretty big," Denise offered, "but we should probably do some segmentation."

"Why would we want to limit ourselves to a smaller market?" Jonathan asked.

"It might make it easier for our Sales Team to focus our efforts," Alex answered tentatively. "Sometimes I think acting too opportunistically causes us to chase the wrong things."

Jonathan had to think for a moment before he responded, because his gut reaction was to get defensive. He liked that their total addressable market was so big—not just because of how it sounded to investors, but because of the number of possibilities it afforded them if they ever wanted to shift their efforts in another direction. He had a hard time believing that it made *more* business sense to go after a *smaller* market.

"A clearer focus would definitely help us in Marketing since we have limited resources," Denise added. She must have sensed Jonathan's hesitation. "We haven't had a chance to dedicate any time to building collateral for the security market yet, even though Alex's team has been pursuing it. It's something I've wanted to do for weeks, but we've just been too short-staffed."

Jonathan nodded. He realized that this must have been the hundredth time that Denise had mentioned needing more staff in Marketing. How had it never seemed like an important issue until now?

He suppressed the urge to sigh at his management issues, and instead turned to Ethan.

"You probably have more information on market, Ethan, but it already sounds like we need a dedicated meeting for that. Can we move to the product?"

Ethan relaxed a bit as he moved to the next slide. "The product hypothesis is really a product brief that covers features, benefits, intellectual property, and stuff like that."

Product Brief

- Product features
- Product benefits
- Intellectual property
- Dependency analysis
- Product delivery schedule
- Total cost of ownership/adoption

6

"Do we have all that?" Alex asked.

"Most of it is in Jonathan's head," Denise quickly responded.

Jonathan smiled slightly before responding. "Yeah, I need to do a better job writing things down, that's for sure."

"That actually kind of stood out as, I guess, a 'key' to customer development; writing down what you believe so that you can test it to see if it's true," Ethan offered cautiously.

"So, is that going to be one of the takeaways," Jonathan started, "that we need to write everything down?"

"Pretty much," Denise offered. "Lean startup, from what I've seen, is about stating what we believe and testing it so that we know we have product/market fit before scaling the company. Without writing it down, we can't test it to confirm what we believe is true."

"Validated learning," Ethan offered.

Jonathan shifted his focus to Denise and asked "Is 'product/market fit' a part of this presentation?"

"It is," Denise responded. "Ethan, can you jump ahead to the last slide of customer validation?"

"Sure," Ethan said as he pressed forward 10 or so slides, past the rest of customer discovery and the slides of customer validation, to a slide labeled 'Product/Market Fit.'"

After a bit of slide show whiplash, everyone paused to read the slide.

Product/Market Fit

- *"You can always feel when product/market fit isn't happening.*
  - The customers aren't quite getting value out of the product,
  - word of mouth isn't spreading,
  - usage isn't growing that fast,
  - press reviews are kind of 'blah',
  - the sales cycle takes too long,
  - and lots of deals never close."

17

"I have to say, that description hits a little close to home." Alex said after reading through the slide. "You might have a future as a writer, Ethan."

"I didn't actually write this," Ethan said. "This is straight from a blog post I found."

After a short pause to confirm there were no additional comments, Ethan moved to the next slide.

Product/Market Fit continued

- *"And you can always feel product/market fit when it's happening.*
  - Customers are buying the product just as fast as you can make it or usage is growing just as fast as you can add more servers.
  - Money from customers is piling up in your checking account.
  - You're hiring sales and customer support staff as fast as you can.
  - Reporters are calling because they've heard about your hot new thing.
  - You start getting entrepreneur of the year awards."

18

"Another direct quote?" Jonathan asked Ethan.

Ethan nodded his head, 'yes.'

Jonathan spent a few moments shaking his head slowly. "Okay, well. I don't know if any of us are qualified to answer this, but how do we get there? Is lean startup the answer to all our problems?"

"It could be," Denise offered. "I don't think we have anything to lose by taking a step or two back and exploring the customer development process."

"We would lose time," Alex offered. "We could spend hours talking about this stuff, and I honestly don't have any idea what we could do differently right now without taking a *huge* step back. I mean, I agree with some of the things that are missing, but I really think we're about to turn a corner with sales, and the tradeshow in Europe next month will create a huge number of opportunities."

"Are you sure about that?" Jonathan asked. He wanted Alex to be sure, of course, because that meant he didn't have to do anything that felt like a big risk for the company. Then he shifted focus to both Denise and Alex. "Do either of you think we'd be able to put our sales back on track without doing anything drastic?"

The room was silent for what seemed like an eternity before Denise spoke up. "Unfortunately, I think the current 'off-track' scenario is pretty well documented. Ethan, can you jump ahead to the new product introduction model slide?"

As everyone turned their attention to Ethan, he skipped forward another six or so slides to one labeled 'The 9 Deadly Sins'."

"9 Deadly Sins" of the New Product Introduction Model

1. Assuming "I Know What the Customer Wants"
2. The "I Know What Features to Build"
3. Focus on Launch Date
4. Emphasis on Execution Instead of Hypotheses, Testing, Learning, and Iteration
5. Traditional Business Plans Presume No Trial and No Errors
6. Confusing Traditional Job Titles with What a Startup Needs to Accomplish
7. Sales and Marketing Execute to a Plan
8. Presumption of Success Leads to Premature Scaling
9. Management by Crisis Leads to a Death Spiral

25

"Not my list, another one I copied from Steve Blank," Ethan offered as everyone read through the sins listed on the screen.

"So, we're on a 'well-documented' path to failure, is what I'm getting here," Jonathan stated. The meeting had been a rollercoaster of hope and disappointment. The tension he felt reminded him of his first coaching session with Helen. "How is this possible? I took the same approach that worked before, but now I'm headed towards a death spiral?"

"Sure is a bit creepy that we are doing most of the things on the list," added Alex. "I mean, not to be discouraging. But it looks like this is the model we've been following lately."

"Well, maybe not number six." Jonathan looked at Denise and asked, "Are we doing number six also?"

"Well, we built functional departments before confirming product/market fit," Denise answered. "Which I know has led to confusion on my end."

"Damn, then we *are* doing everything on the list," Jonathan said, exasperated. "There has to be some steps we can take to get out of this situation. Is that what's on the next slide?"

Ethan laughed nervously. He didn't move forward to the next slide.

"We can," Denise started, straightening up in her chair a bit, "but I honestly don't have the bandwidth to add another priority to my current list of priorities. We would have to stop something in order to start following this customer development process. Either that, or I need more resources. Until one of those things happens, we're stuck where we are."

"I'd be willing to give up one of my open positions if it would help move this forward," Alex added. "This is the kind of stuff my team is begging for. I think it would make our jobs easier if we had product/market fit."

"Okay, now we're getting into a different discussion," Jonathan said. "Let's finish up with Ethan and then we can get into that for a few minutes before I have a call with some engineers at Halskee. Any other questions or comments for Ethan?"

Denise was the first to respond, "No questions from me." She practically beamed at her intern. "I think he's done a great job putting all this together on such short notice."

"Yes, great work," both Jonathan and Alex agreed.

"I know it's only 5:30pm, but you've earned the rest of the day off," Jonathan said with a smile. "I promise you'll get more of a heads-up next time I give you an assignment. I don't like what I found out, but it's *definitely* what we needed to hear, so, *great job.*"

"Thanks," Ethan floundered a little bit. "And, I mean, the presentation wasn't too bad. Startups are way cooler than the kind of company I was working for last summer."

"Well, great," Jonathan responded. "Because we could definitely use the help."

Ethan left the conference room, and hopefully went straight home to get some sleep, while Jonathan led Alex and Denise through a short discussion of the pros and cons of delaying a Sales hire to put resources on customer development. Making the change would require an adjustment to the quota number that Alex's team would be responsible for, but that seemed a moot point, seeing as they weren't on track anyway with their current resources and, apparently, the company had been committing *deadly sins*.

Jonathan thought about how a few simple questions in a coaching meeting and a presentation by an MBA intern had managed to make him want to completely rethink the sales and marketing strategy.

"It's starting to look like we need to focus more on marketing than sales at this point," he finally admitted out loud to his team, and to himself. "I mean, we've only scratched the surface on what customer discovery is and haven't even started to talk about the other steps."

He looked over at Denise. "I have a feeling we're going to need even more resources in Marketing if we want to tackle the goal of getting things back on track."

"Definitely," Denise replied. "Switching from the new product introduction model to lean startup is a big undertaking.

"In the short research I've done, customer discovery and validation make a lot of sense if you ask me," she continued, "I feel like we shortchanged both seven months ago after you hired Alex and stopped visiting customers."

She glanced over at Alex and added, "No offense, Alex."

"What do you mean?" Jonathan asked.

"Customer discovery takes in-depth learning about our customer's problems and how we can solve them with our product. You were learning a lot about what customers needed, but it went straight from your head and into the product. I never got a chance to participate in what you were learning. Now I spend all of my time creating collateral that seems disconnected."

Jonathan shifted his focus to look at Alex. "Am I the only one whose head is spinning?"

"No, but I think we're all starting to spin in the right direction. This is the best conversation we've had as a leadership team since I joined SyncAnalytix." Alex started to push away from the conference table, and he almost looked disappointed to leave the meeting this time. "I wish I didn't have to break up this meeting already, but I need to get to a dinner reservation, or I'll be sleeping on the couch tonight. You know how it goes."

Even in the acknowledgement that they were short-staffed, and underperforming, and had a whole lot of work to do, Jonathan had never seen his VP of Sales and Director of Marketing look so motivated. And he realized, with a start, that he really wanted to tell Helen about the whole thing.

"I need to go as well or I'll be late for the Halskee call," Jonathan said as he stood up. Then he paused and looked over to Denise.

"I know it's short notice and you have a lot on your plate, but chances are the Halskee engineers will talk about some of their needs. Can you join me on the call and see what we can learn?"

"Yes!" Denise answered without missing a beat.

It was the most energy Jonathan had seen in her since they first started working together. Maybe he had learned something from Helen, already.

8
DEADLY SINS

"What did you learn from your team last week?" was Helen's first question after Jonathan settled into his seat in the conference room.

After Ethan's presentation and the discussions that followed, Jonathan felt eager to sit down with Helen and get her input on all of it.

"A lot," he said. This time he made sure to put his phone in airplane mode before turning it upside down on the table.

Helen, mirroring Jonathan's own excitement, encouraged him to continue.

"I don't even know where to start," Jonathan said. "So much has happened in the past few days, I should've created an outline so I could make sure not to leave anything out."

Helen smiled, clearly amused and maybe even proud at seeing such a major shift in Jonathan's attitude since their first encounter, way back at the C-IQ event. Jonathan couldn't believe it had only been a few weeks since then.

"I'm sure you'll remember to tell me all the key points."

"Like the fact that my company is in the middle of a death spiral," Jonathan began. He had to mention *that* key point sooner or later, although it was a little harder to be light-hearted about it. "I thought we were on a roller coaster, but it turns out we are on a well-known—and *well-documented*—death spiral."

"What do you mean by that?" Helen asked. "A 'well-known death spiral'?"

Jonathan sat back and collected his thoughts. With all the activity at SyncAnalytix, Jonathan hadn't had much time to process things on his own after Ethan's presentation. He was grateful he'd already had this meeting scheduled beforehand.

"Okay. Maybe 'well-known' is a bit flippant. I just really don't know how else to characterize the situation when the Marketing team points out exactly what's wrong with SyncAnalytix by just copying straight from a book that's been out for years."

"And what was your big takeaway from what your Marketing team pointed out?" Helen asked.

"That *I'm* the problem, not Alex."

Helen nodded slowly at that, as if she wasn't entirely convinced. "I think I need some more information here. The last time we spoke, you thought the reason the company was missing quota was because your team didn't have a clear sales strategy. Now you're the problem?"

"I'm the reason for the death spiral," Jonathan said. He made a downward spiral motion with his right index finger.

"Are you able to share what led you to this conclusion?" Helen prompted.

"To be honest, what I learned came from Denise and her intern, Ethan. It turns out that Ethan's capstone project is on lean startup and how things like customer discovery apply to technology startups."

"Startups like SyncAnalytix?" Helen asked.

"Exactly," Jonathan continued. "I asked him to research and put together a presentation on customer discovery since I had heard the term from Vaughn but didn't really know what it meant."

Jonathan paused to see if Helen was still tracking. When she nodded an affirmative, he elaborated further.

"So, customer discovery is different from traditional new product development. That's what I'm good at, the traditional process. It's what I did at BlackBee that led to our successful exit."

"Is there something wrong with SyncAnalytix following the traditional process?" Helen asked.

Jonathan tried to think of how exactly they'd phrased it during their meeting.

"I can't remember if Ethan said it or if it came up later in discussions with Denise, but I think the challenge is that the traditional process assumes that the customer problem is well-understood, and the product features are well-known. Customer discovery is what people do when that stuff is not known."

"How would you describe SyncAnalytix when it comes to understanding the customer problem and the product features?" Helen asked.

Jonathan leaned back in his chair and thought back to when he told Ethan that he 'knew better than customers' when it came to what they needed. Looking back, it seemed like an arrogant statement.

"Well, if you had asked me last week, I would have told you that I already know what customers need, so asking them would be a waste of time. Now I'm not so sure. I thought we were going to win a partnership in the security market, now it looks like we will need to reduce our price to a point where it really doesn't make sense for us to even bid."

"What would assure you that you know what the customer needs?" Helen asked.

"When they buy our product," Jonathan said. He shook his head slightly, a little put off by the question. But then he remembered that he'd already been wrong about this before.

"Actually, I think that's what the whole customer discovery process is about. Ethan had some slides on a step he called customer validation, but we skipped over that stuff in the interest of time."

Helen let there be silence to see if Jonathan had any further thoughts.

"Would it be ok to reflect back what I think I've heard you say over the past few minutes?" Helen asked.

Jonathan nodded.

"A challenge with the traditional product development process is that it assumes you know what the customer needs. This new process, customer discovery, attempts to fix that by doing something called validation. You aren't sure that you know what the customer needs, so you've been depending on sales to confirm that you created a valuable product." Helen paused before asking, "Does that sound correct?".

"Well, that *is* what I said, minus the death spiral part," Jonathan said. "When you say it, I wonder, 'Why don't we just try the customer discovery thing?' Is that your next question?"

Helen smiled, causing Jonathan to believe his assertion was correct.

"Well, I'll tell you why," Jonathan continued, "because I don't know anything about this customer discovery thing. We've already launched our product, we have a quota to meet, and we have investor expectations to meet."

Jonathan felt tension flooding into his system again, just listing those three things off. He closed his eyes, tilted his head down, and shook his head slowly from left to right and back again.

"Are you willing to share what's going through your mind right now?" Helen asked cautiously.

"Yeah, that I just gave you two reasons that are two of the nine deadly sins. Number nine is the death spiral, by the way."

Jonathan continued to move his chin slowly from left to right, deep in thought.

"The truth is, I don't know where to start. I can't go to the board and say we're restarting the company because an intern made a presentation. And what about the tradeshow coming up in Europe?"

Jonathan began to get a sinking feeling down in his stomach; from the realization that all the time being spent getting his company ready for the tradeshow might now be wasted, but also from the thought that pulling out at the last minute might damage his reputation. He tried one more time to make his case for the original plan.

"I'll lose credibility if we pull out of the show now," Jonathan argued. "And anyway, I wouldn't know where to start on this customer discovery thing. What are we supposed to do—meet with customers, conduct focus groups and interviews? I don't even know what questions to ask. I can't turn the sales and marketing strategy of the company over to an unknown process. We would need more help to do something like that. Expert help, probably."

"Who do you know who could help you with customer discovery?" Helen asked.

"That's just it, I don't know anyone who's an expert in customer discovery."

Helen paused for a moment, and then prompted him another time,

"If you knew someone who might know, who might that person be?"

Jonathan looked at Helen and shook his head in disbelief.

"It doesn't matter how many different ways you ask me the same question; I don't know anyone."

Then Jonathan stopped shaking his head and his eyes got wide.

"But Amir might. I go heads-down when I start a company, but he somehow stays connected to the startup community. If anyone knows someone who might be an expert, it would be Amir."

"Are you willing to call Amir to see if he can help you find an expert?" Helen asked.

"Sure," Jonathan answered. "I've been meaning to grab coffee with him since I saw him at your C-IQ talk."

Helen looked satisfied with that answer. Jonathan just hoped that reaching out to Amir might get him somewhere, since it seemed like his coach would only continue to ask him more questions. Speaking of which…

"We still have a few minutes left today, is there anything else we can discuss that will help you feel like you're making progress?" she asked next.

Jonathan thought for a second.

"I don't know if I'm going to feel like I've made any progress until I've figured out what I'm missing on customer discovery. I guess I'm pretty anxious to get started with that question."

"You have a plan to contact Amir to see if he knows anyone. If for some reason Amir doesn't know anyone, who else could you ask?"

"I guess I could ask Denise," Jonathan answered. "It seems like she knows what customer discovery means, which means she might know someone who could help."

"Is there any reason to not ask either Amir or Denise?"

Jonathan thought for a minute. During Ethan's presentation, it was clear that Denise had some knowledge about lean startup and customer discovery that she hadn't shared before. Why didn't Jonathan just ask her at that meeting if there was someone who could help them through the process?

"Sometimes," Jonathan began tentatively. He sighed. "I guess the truth is that sometimes it feels awkward to ask my team for help."

Helen paused Sensing he had some more to process, Helen asked, "can you tell me more about that? Why would asking your team for help feel awkward?"

"As the founder and CEO, shouldn't I have the answers?" Jonathan responded. "I mean, especially in this case. I've probably *told* people we're following lean startup and that our first product was an MVP. Now, all of a sudden, I don't even know what lean startup means. It's embarrassing."

"It's hard to be an expert in everything," Helen offered. "Are you willing to let go of being the expert in order to ask for the help you need?"

Jonathan let out an even longer sigh, leaned back in his chair, and then ran both hands over his hair and grasped the back of his head.

"That's who I am; I'm the expert. It's my identity. I mean, I can joke about it, make sarcastic comments that people think are funny because they know how smart I am, but to really, seriously ask for help, I don't know how to do that. That must be how I ended up in this mess."

"What if you *did* know how to do that?" Helen said, with a look on her face that Jonathan could only describe as a respectful smirk.

"Now, that's funny," Jonathan laughed. "I guess one of my commitments is about to be 'let go of being the expert.'"

"Being transparent about not having all the answers can lead to deeper connections and build more trust with your team. It's hard to work as a team if everyone feels they don't measure up to the leader."

"Can you recommend a way to get started with 'not being the expert,' other than asking Denise for help?" Jonathan asked.

"It could be something as simple as not giving all the answers, asking for the input of others before you respond, or being open to the ideas of others."

"Ok," Jonathan said as he raised both hands in a display of surrender. "I can give that a try and ask Denise for an expert if Amir doesn't have any ideas."

"And how will you let me know once you have found an expert on customer discovery?"

"I can send an email once Amir tells me who he knows," Jonathan said with confidence.

Jonathan had a feeling he was getting better at this whole coaching thing.

9
STAYING CONNECTED

"Jonathan," Amir called out as soon as he entered the coffee shop. Jonathan was near the door picking up his drink from the counter.

Even with how much both of them had on their plates now compared to when they were at Meranti, Amir and Jonathan managed to find time to meet within just a week of Jonathan reaching out. That had to be a schedule coordination record. Which must have been what Amir was thinking, too.

"Two Jonathan Reeves sightings in one month," he said. "If we keep this up it'll be just like the old days."

"It's great to see you, too." Jonathan could feel himself reflecting Amir's enthusiasm already. "I wish I remembered how you take your coffee. I would have ordered one for you."

Amir smiled. "No worries, I'm sure it's changed since Meranti Ventures. Mid-morning, I switch to decaf. Doctor's orders." He laughed, waving Jonathan away from the counter. "You grab us a table, and I'll order."

Jonathan checked his phone while he waited for Amir to get through the line, scrolling through his overflowing inbox and worrying, again, that he should be doing something else right now.

He didn't have too much time to think about it, though, before Amir sat down in the chair next to him.

Jonathan wasn't much for small talk even when he didn't have an agenda, but seeing Amir brought back a flood of fond memories. His infectious optimism, which, admittedly, got old when they worked in the same building, was only entertaining now. Jonathan realized he wouldn't mind catching up, as much as he was in a hurry to ask for Amir's help.

"It was great seeing you the other night at the event," Jonathan began. "I wish I did a better job of staying in touch with people. How have you been doing?"

Amir smiled and shared what he had been up to the past few years since they both left Meranti. He had been part of the growth equity team and identified a rollup opportunity. After months of research and identifying the right platform, the investment committee approved the funds for the acquisition, and Amir was off to the races.

Jonathan was a technologist, some might say inventor, though nowadays he preferred entrepreneur. Growth by acquisition was an exciting field he knew little about. While he listened to Amir recount the past few years, he wondered if Amir would know anything about customer discovery.

"That's what I've been up to," Amir concluded. "I mean, workwise. If you wanted to know everything else I've got going on we'd be here all day. And you'd get bored at some point.

"So," he cleared his throat and shifted his tone of voice. Jonathan was always impressed by how quickly he could change gears like that. "Tell me about you and SyncAnalytix—and did you decide to meet with Helen after all?"

Before Jonathan could really think about how he wanted to respond or where he wanted to start, someone who knew Amir stopped by their table to say 'hi.'. It shouldn't have come as a surprise that someone outside the office knew Amir, since he was so friendly. After brief introductions and some small talk, Amir's visitor left, and they were able to continue their conversation.

"Sorry, where were we?" Amir asked.

"I was about to tell you more about SyncAnalytix," Jonathan replied, "and whether or not I decided to meet with Helen."

Jonathan brought Amir up to date on the SyncAnalytix experience and recent Series A funding. Even though Amir asked directly (again), he avoided going into detail regarding the discussions with Halskee and whether or not there was an opportunity to get acquired in the near future.

"And yes, I guess you could say Helen is my executive coach now," Jonathan added. "At least, we've met twice already. I'm not sure what to think about the process. It seems like she asks a bunch of questions and doesn't give me any answers."

Amir let out a big laugh. "Yeah, I can see where an engineer would have trouble with executive coaching if you're expecting answers from your coach. I bet you've asked her a few times to just tell you the answer, haven't you?"

"Am I that predictable?"

"Yes and no," Amir continued. "I remember you like everything black and white before you move forward on anything. Sometimes when I meet with my coach, I wonder, *'Is this even a rhetorical question?'* because it feels like they know the answer and won't tell me."

This time it was Jonathan who laughed. "Exactly!"

"Yeah, that's not how it works," Amir responded, shaking his head. "A *good* coach will figure out how to help you pull the information out of your head. Sometimes we know the answer but are afraid to act for some reason or another. At least, that's what I've noticed my coach helps with more than anything."

"To be honest it's a little frustrating sometimes. And it seems like it isn't going to get any less frustrating."

Even talking to Amir about it made Jonathan feel echoes of his last meeting with Helen. He wasn't in denial anymore that coaching was something he needed. But if he needed it, why did it bother him so much?

"Well, it'll probably feel like that for a while. Especially when you come to the realization that *you* are the source of most of your problems."

Jonathan's eyes got big and then he took a deep breath. Suddenly it was as if the entire coffee shop around them had quieted down. "So, it's not just me."

"Nope, it happens to the best of us." Amir smiled and patted Jonathan on the shoulder. "Welcome to the life of an executive."

Jonathan let out a sigh of relief. "Alright, you seem to know this coaching thing pretty well. Maybe you can help with this weird question Helen asked me last time we met."

"A weird question, huh. I can certainly try," Amir said as a slight smirk came across his face, "but I bet you actually know the answer."

"That's just it. I don't. We were talking about needing to do customer discovery and she asked, 'Do you know anyone who can help?' I said 'no' because I don't. Then she asked, 'if you knew someone who might know, who would it be?' Is that some kind of mind trick?"

Amir thought it over for a second. "That *is* a funny one. Maybe it would help to specify what kind of customer discovery help you need."

"I really don't know. I don't even know what customer discovery is. All I know is that we don't have product/market fit and I need to fix that fast."

Amir let out a little snort, looking at Jonathan as if this was some sort of inside joke. He was as cryptic as Helen, apparently; he just had a sense of humor about it.

"What now?" Jonathan asked. "This is serious, I was hoping you might actually know someone."

Amir broke into a full-on laugh as if he found what Jonathan had just said hysterical.

"I'm sorry," Amir said as he tried to compose himself. "It's just that you *do* know the person you're looking for."

"No, I don't."

"Parth Ansari, remember? If anyone knows product/market fit, it's got to be Parth. The guy is a PMF coach. I mean literally; a product - market - fit - coach." Amir said, emphasizing each word.

"Parth from Meranti?" Jonathan asked. "I thought he was doing marketing technology startups or something."

"Back then, yeah, but when this whole lean startup thing happened, he switched his focus. Call him right now. He was the CMO for a few successful startups and then went independent."

Jonathan hastily reached for his phone and then looked back at Amir. "I have a meeting later this week to finalize plans for the tradeshow. If we are really going to give this customer discovery thing a try, I need to know now.

"But do I really need another coach?"

Amir nodded "He's a different type of coach," Amir continued, "probably more like an expert consultant. I bet his number is the same, give him a call. I mean, what have you got to lose?"

Jonathan searched through his contacts for Parth's number and hit the call button before he could have second thoughts about it.

"My reputation, probably. Maybe my entire company."

Amir gave him a thumbs-up. Parth answered on the third ring.

"Jonathan Reeves!" he said in a booming voice. "It must be my lucky day. To what do I owe the pleasure of this phone call?"

"Hi Parth," Jonathan smiled. Parth sounded like he hadn't changed at all since his days working in marketing at technology startups. "I'm sitting here with Amir Rubin and your name came up. We were talking about who I might know who knows customer discovery, and here I am on the phone with you. Did I call the right guy?" he asked.

"Actually, yes," Parth said. "I do have a lot of experience in that area. It wasn't very big back in our Meranti Ventures days, but it's come a long way since."

"I was hoping you could help me figure out where my company is in that process," Jonathan added.

"I can definitely try my best to help you with "crossing the chasm," as it's called. Did you want to talk about it now or schedule a time?"

"Honestly, I know this is out of the blue, but the sooner we can meet, the better. I have some tough decisions coming up, and I would really appreciate your input."

"That's funny timing," Parth responded. "I just had a lunch meeting cancel for tomorrow and I was contemplating what to do with my reservation at La Perla's at noon."

"I can meet you for lunch tomorrow," Jonathan said, "if you don't mind me filling in."

"Let's do it," Parth responded.

"Great! I'll see you then."

Jonathan hung up and looked at Amir. "Lunch tomorrow with Parth. Wait, do you have any lunch plans tomorrow? You should come."

"Unfortunately, I can't join you guys. I would love to, but I have a working lunch with our banker and legal counsel. I doubt it will be as exciting as your meeting with Parth." Amir smiled, still chuckling from earlier. "And it certainly won't be as fun as the past twenty minutes. We better get going, I bet you have a lot of work waiting for you back at the office."

"Let's do this again soon," Jonathan said as they both got up from the table. "It was great to catch-up, and you actually did help me out with that coaching question."

"Try not to sound so surprised," Amir replied with a hint of sarcasm.

"It never occurred to me that there's even a job title of product/market fit coach. How do you keep up with what everyone's doing?"

"I see stuff here and there on social media," Amir explained as they walked back to their cars, "but mostly from meetings like this, just keeping in touch with people from time to time."

"Maybe I should do more of that."

"Definitely! And good luck with Parth. I'm looking forward to hearing how it goes."

"If it's anything like my current experience with coaching, it'll be a bunch of questions I don't know the answers to."

"Or a bunch of questions you *thought* you didn't know the answers to," Amir countered with a wry smile.

"Or that." Jonathan laughed as he shook Amir's hand goodbye. "I'll let you know."

10
PMF COACH

"Parth, it's great to see you again," Jonathan said as soon as he arrived at the table. He'd only had to tell the hostess Parth's first name and she immediately took him through the restaurant. At the table was a well-dressed man who looked exactly how Jonathan remembered him. Even though he was pretty sure that was at least three years ago.

Parth had been an Entrepreneur-in-Residence at Meranti Ventures before Jonathan sold BlackBee. He'd already transitioned out by the time Jonathan came in, but they knew of each other through their association with Meranti and had run into each other at a couple of events. Jonathan had little knowledge of his career since then, but he still hoped Amir was right that Parth was the person to go to for help.

"Sorry I'm late," Jonathan added as he reached out to shake Parth's hand.

"Hey, don't worry about it!" Parth replied, standing up for a moment to shake Jonathan's hand. Jonathan took a seat across from him. "Plus, I would have been eating alone anyway if you hadn't offered to fill-in."

"I'm actually really glad you had time to meet on such short notice," Jonathan began, "I'm in a tough spot right now and need to make a quick decision. I'm hoping you might have some input on whether you think I'm on the right track."

"Well, that's a lot of pressure for a lunch meeting," Parth joked, but he didn't seem to be turned off by the weight of Jonathan's expectations for their meeting. "Let's order first and then you can tell me more about what's going on."

Jonathan reviewed the menu for a few minutes until the waiter returned to ask if they had any questions. Finally, he decided on the lunch special, while Parth told the waiter he would have "the usual."

"You must come here often if the waiter knows what your usual order is."

"Probably more than I should," Parth admitted. "Although I'm one of the owners, after all."

"CEO of one of the top marketing technology startups *and* a restaurateur," Jonathan noted. "Interesting resume."

"Ha!" Parth gave a deep belly laugh. "I've never heard those two in the same sentence before. I'd say I'm more of a product/market fit coach-by-day, restaurateur-by-night. Or in this case, by lunch break." He laughed again.

Jonathan just nodded. He could imagine getting to the end of this lunch and realizing they'd spent the entire hour just catching up. He'd forgotten how social the man was. Thankfully, Parth seemed to remember that Jonathan was on a schedule.

"So, tell me how I can assist you with my customer discovery experience."

"I'm not even sure where to start," Jonathan responded.

"Well, you mentioned customer discovery on the phone, but let's start with that 'quick decision' you need to make. That might be a good place."

"Right." Jonathan thought for a moment on how he could explain the situation without wasting any time. "We're scheduled to exhibit at a tradeshow in Munich in a few weeks, and it's been on the calendar for a long time. But Sales keeps missing its forecasts, and I've finally come to realize that Marketing doesn't have nearly enough resources, and now, I'm starting to wonder if a tradeshow in Europe is the right thing to be doing with our time and money right now," Jonathan answered, feeling a bit winded from unloading it all.

He took a breath. "We have a meeting this afternoon to finalize plans for the tradeshow, and now I'm considering canceling the whole thing. Is that crazy?"

Parth did not respond right away but instead paused for a moment before asking,

"Do you think you could explain where you are with marketing? I don't want to make any assumptions about what you mean by 'not enough resources' in Marketing."

"I thought I had a handle on marketing at SyncAnalytix." Jonathan sighed. "I mean, I *thought* I knew what we were doing, but when our growth stalled and a board member asked if it was the right time for the sales strategy we've been following, I just didn't have a good answer.

"I met with my Director of Marketing only to find out that she might be capable of the kind of discovery work that could support sales this whole time, but she just doesn't have the resources. She has a little help right now, at least, since we brought on an intern. They gave an assessment of where we are, but that's just based on a few lean startup textbooks. Even then, the outlook of that was pretty bleak."

Jonathan decided not to mention the whole 'death spiral' part.

"And one of the conclusions we came to was that we completely shortchanged the customer discovery process. I still hardly know what *customer discovery* even entails."

"I don't know if this will make you feel better, but I've definitely seen entrepreneurs go through this same situation before," Parth said. Something about his calm demeanor regarding SyncAnalytix's situation actually *did* make Jonathan feel better.

"Yeah, and we're too short-staffed to even get into trying to fix it. So here I am." Jonathan took a moment to collect his thoughts. Ever since his last meeting with Denise, any time the issue of marketing came up, his mind would immediately start running

"I have a Sales Team that's struggling, and I don't know where the problem is. I have a Marketing Team that could be doing more but I don't know where to pull the additional resources from. Do I have the wrong sales strategy, the wrong marketing strategy, or both? My first thought was just to replace the Sales VP after we kept missing quota but talking to my team has made me wonder if *I* should actually be doing something else to get us back on track—and if that something else includes pulling out of the tradeshow."

"Sounds like you *are* in a tough spot," Parth said as the waiter brought out their meals. "I'd love to know if there's any sort of wisdom I could offer you that would help."

"Well, hold on. This looks great," Jonathan said, watching the plate being set on the table in front of him. "To be honest, I think I want to take a break from talking about SyncAnalytix while I eat this salmon."

"Works for me," Parth responded with a smile.

Over the next few minutes Parth and Jonathan made small talk as they enjoyed their lunch. Jonathan learned more about Parth and his background in marketing. Working for various startups in Silicon Valley before settling in San Diego. Jonathan shared his technical background and what had brought him to where he was now with SyncAnalytix. Multiple startups, a quick sale, and a successful exit. Jonathan admitted that he was confused how he'd ended up in such an uncertain state after what had seemed like a successful start to his career.

"So, I guess that's also one of my concerns," Jonathan added, circling back to their earlier conversation. "What will my board think if I back out of this tradeshow? Will they think I've lost it and that my first exit was an anomaly?"

"It would be incorrect—not to mention unproductive—to talk about startups as if they're all the same," Parth started. "My experience says each one is different. Your board members would probably agree. But I still think it's helpful to have a framework to refer to while you lead your company through the different stages of finding product/market fit. It may be that your previous startup just happened upon product/market fit by complete coincidence."

"That could explain why this all seems new to me," Jonathan said. "Of course, I've *heard* people talk about lean startup, product/market fit, and all that, but I don't think I've ever had to work so hard to figure it out. BlackBee was a technology improvement in the machine-to-machine market. What we're doing now with IoT is different, and honestly, sometimes I wonder if the market exists yet."

Parth nodded. "Creating new markets is tough for startups. Maybe tougher than new technology," he explained. "The tools for customer discovery and building things like awareness and preference in order to make the transition from early adopters to the mainstream market have developed over the years, but they're just that: *tools*. Part of leading an early-stage startup is to know when to use the right tools and when to ask the right questions of your team."

"Now that you mention it, I did feel like my team was holding back once I started asking different questions." Jonathan paused, then added, "Or any questions. I think for a while I was just trying not to interfere. I figured they would tell me everything I needed to know about what they were doing, so if they didn't tell me something, that meant everything was on track."

Parth smiled. He must have heard that from entrepreneurs before, too.

"Everyone is busy doing the tactical work in a startup. Getting employees to think strategically isn't easy when their day is consumed with what feels like an endless list of tasks. It is much easier to focus on execution than discovery." Parth glanced at his watch. "But I may be getting us off track. What piece of the puzzle be missing for the decision you need to make about the tradeshow?"

"I have one question that you could seriously help with: is now the right time to spend money on scaling, or do I have more important marketing work to do first?"

"Okay, well, we probably don't have time to answer a question *that* broad," Parth admitted, holding his hands up in surrender. "What's your gut feeling?"

"I feel like there's still work to do in understanding who our ideal customer is," Jonathan answered, "More than I thought, and that seems like it should be my priority. But I don't want to cancel everything based on my gut."

"Why do you feel like there's more work to do in understanding your customer?"

Jonathan took a deep breath.

"Six months ago, I thought the product was ready to go to market. Now I'm really not sure anymore. There seems to be misalignment here and there, and that's probably what makes the sales process so much harder than I think it should be. At first, I thought we just had the wrong Sales leader, but after I started digging deeper, it looks like we left some key things undone. In the past, I would just design a product to meet what I knew was a market need. I would tell Marketing, 'Here's where the customers are, make sure they know about our product,' and I would tell Sales, 'This is our product; go sell it.'"

Jonathan paused and reflected for a moment, wondering if they were making any progress towards answering his question about the tradeshow. He started to worry.

"Yes," Parth said. "Things used to be much easier. Still complicated, but easier. When customers, markets, and business models are well known, there are clear processes for executing. Complicated processes, still, but nothing compared to the complexity of identifying unknown customers and creating new markets."

Jonathan could relate to the complexity of identifying unknown customers.

"The complexity of both markets and products has increased, and now Marketing has had to build tools and processes for addressing what used to be simpler," Parth continued, "Customer development is one of the newer tools that has taken on a life of its own as *Lean Startup*. I like to think of these tools as 'communication enablers' for my team."

Jonathan felt his stomach turn as he thought about the fact that he'd already determined, for certain, that SyncAnalytix was trying to follow a completely different model. Probably the *wrong* model for their circumstances.

"Is there a tool that tells you when you are spending the right money on the right things in marketing?" Jonathan asked.

"Yes and no," Parth replied. "The challenge is no longer as simple as measuring the efficacy of your advertising dollars. You need a framework dedicated to what your company is trying to accomplish at each stage. One that doesn't just address deploying capital on the right things, but deploying it at the right time, too."

"Exactly," Jonathan agreed. "If I had something like that already in place, then I guess I wouldn't be struggling with this decision about the tradeshow. And I probably wouldn't have to wait until the last minute to make a decision, either" he laughed, trying to shake off some of his anxiety.

"You'll still need to make some tough tradeoffs, no matter what," Parth continued, "but it would help to have the decision process be more aligned with your strategy, and to be able to track results against your strategy, too. So, who is your ideal customer?"

Jonathan remembered the idea of having a customer persona from one of Ethan's slides, but he hadn't spent any time thinking about it since that meeting. He paused.

Finally, he answered, "Someone who wants to add data analytics to their monitoring dashboard. But I have a feeling that this isn't specific enough to be of any help, and it doesn't really sound like a customer persona."

"It's a start," Parth said, "and sometimes a simple strategy is what works to get the ball rolling. I've seen companies make simple descriptions work when they are in known markets with known sales processes. The startups that are going after new markets often need a more specific vision targeting a minimum viable market. They need to articulate what they believe will happen and then test and validate it as quickly and cheaply as possible."

Jonathan reflected for a moment, thinking back to his last startup when things ran so much more smoothly. BlackBee quickly reached $2M in annual revenue, but most of the revenue came through a value-added reseller, and 80% of that revenue came from one customer. That customer then acquired BlackBee soon after a successful implementation with their core product. All those connections, from the value-added reseller to the strategic customer, came from the VP of Sales; very little effort was put into marketing.

"I'm ashamed to admit it, but I don't know where to start when it comes to creating a marketing strategy, and I still don't know what customer discovery is. I guess I've always relied on the people I hire to be responsible for what they do."

"That's very common," Parth said. "Founders will hire the expertise they need to fill out their team but will not think to direct those team members strategically—or are afraid to try to. You probably know more marketing strategy and customer discovery than you give yourself credit for. The challenge may be taking the strategy out of your head and sharing it with your team. I would recommend sitting down with your team for a few days and working through a full discussion of your strategy."

"I don't know if we *have* a few days just to talk about strategy. Even the changes we talked about making in our last meeting have been slow-going because of how much work there is to do."

"Taking the time to fully assess your company and your team's expectations probably sounds like more trouble than it's worth right now," Parth agreed, "but you'll actually save time in the long run if everyone is on the same page, and you have a clear strategy for finding product/market fit."

"Otherwise," Jonathan interrupted, thinking out loud, "we keep spinning our wheels hoping for the best."

Parth nodded. "Exactly."

"Six months ago, I thought I knew how things were going to play out," Jonathan responded. "Now I don't even know why I had the expectations that I did. Or if I had any clear expectations at all."

Jonathan paused as he thought about some of the conversations between Marketing and Sales, and the most recent challenges bidding against OscarIoT.

"Well, I think you just answered my question about the tradeshow. We're not all on the same page. Only now I'm wondering how I can get us there, especially with the issue of customer discovery."

"You need to take the lead," Parth replied. "Sounds like you have a meeting this afternoon with Marketing and Sales Teams to talk about the tradeshow. You could use that time to brainstorm with your team instead. Just see what everyone has to say about the business needs, technological requirements, and goals that your customer has regarding the problem they need to solve. There is a lot of information out there on how to build a useful strategy for your startup, but honestly the best thing you can do is just take what's in your head and put it on a whiteboard for everyone to see."

"That sounds like a mess," Jonathan said, feeling his eyes go wide at Parth's suggestion. "I'll definitely need more structure otherwise we'll end up talking for hours from twenty different directions on all the possible options for the product."

"Ha! You certainly are an engineer, aren't you?" Parth smiled, leaning back in his chair. "If you need more structure than that, I really recommend taking multiple days to talk through every step of the process: what is your market, who is your customer, what is the problem they are trying to solve, what are they willing to pay for your solution, and how you can develop a strategy with the highest probability for success. If your team can reach a consensus on all of those topics, you'll avoid situations in the future where something *feels* wrong, but you don't know why."

"Multiple days, huh?"

"That's what I recommend when I come in to moderate those discussions," Parth added.

That gave Jonathan an idea.

"Can you come in and walk us through that discussion? We need to get things back on track as soon as possible."

"We might be able to get something on the calendar soon, provided that you and your team can unplug for a few days." Parth looked thoughtful for a second, like he was visualizing his own calendar in his mind.

"We can make that happen," Jonathan responded enthusiastically. Even the idea of scheduling this meeting with Parth and his team felt like taking multiple steps in the right direction.

Feeling a sense of completion, Jonathan looked around for the waiter, hoping that he could grab the check before Parth did. He couldn't seem to spot the guy. Finally, he turned back to Parth.

"I really appreciate you letting me take your open lunch spot. I'd like to grab the check before I get going, but I think our waiter's gone on break."

"You're very welcome," Parth replied. "And the waitstaff here knows not to bother bringing a bill to one of the owners.

Jonathan was surprised at first, but then realized it made sense. "I guess I never really thought about what it means to own a restaurant," he said. "Thanks for lunch as well."

"I'm glad things worked out in our schedules. The process of developing a strategy for finding product/market fit can be tough at times, but I've seen it work wonders."

Parth started to get up from the table. "I need to head back to the office for a meeting, and you probably need a head-start on your next meeting as well."

Jonathan got up after him. He was thinking about at least ten different things at once, most of them related to his next meeting, but he started to look forward to the possibility of having a dedicated strategy meeting like Parth mentioned. He was already curious what would come out of it, and what he'd hear from Alex and Denise when he asked them to share their own perspectives.

"Best of luck this afternoon with your meeting," Parth said, pulling Jonathan out of his thoughts as he shook his hand to say goodbye. "Engage your team more on this stuff; you won't be sorry."

"I'll do what I can," Jonathan replied. "Thanks again for your help, I'm starting to feel better about what I need to do."

"Well, you certainly look less tense than when you sat down," Parth added, smiling wide. "Practicing customer discovery to the point of generating effective sales can take months, but I think you're on the right track, even if it doesn't feel like it yet. I look forward to hearing about your progress. And let me know when you want to schedule time for us to walk through a product/market fit strategy with your team."

Jonathan nodded and made his way out of the restaurant. Everything Parth had said towards the end of their lunch had been encouraging, but there was one word that started to tug at his mind: *months.*

Months? he thought, walking to his car, *how will I explain that to the board?*

He knew two things for certain: He had to pull SyncAnalytix out of the tradeshow, and he had to get this strategy session scheduled with Parth as soon as possible.

11
FIFTEEN MINUTES

As much as he'd tried to forget about it, Jonathan drove through the city with the word 'months' rattling around in his brain. *I don't have that kind of time to get things where they need to be*, he thought, *there has to be a faster way*.

When he reached his office, he sank into his chair, already starting to doubt whether he could pull this off. He needed more time to decompress and gather his thoughts before the 2pm meeting, time to put together a cohesive strategy and a presentation to sell it. Fifteen minutes was all he had.

As he contemplated how to make the best use of what little time he *did* have to prepare, his computer and phone chimed simultaneously. Jonathan reached for his phone on instinct—it was probably the developers communicating over chat—but he stopped himself. They could wait, at least until after his meeting.

Jonathan switched his phone to airplane mode and turned off the speakers on his computer before he could even speculate what the notification from his desktop could have been. He pushed his chair back from his desk, closed his eyes, and took a few deep breaths. If there was ever a time when he needed to calm his thoughts and practice some mindfulness, it was now.

But Jonathan's mind continued to race. From one open loop to another, he bounced from development challenges to sales calls to

Marketing meetings, and eventually circled back to his last conversations with Parth and Helen. He spent so much of his time operating in this way, following his thoughts wherever they went, that he had trouble calming down. Each time he realized he was distracted, he tried to refocus on his breath.

Breathe in… Hold…

We need to get those three story points deployed or the new feature won't work for Halskee, he thought.

No, not now. Breathe in… Hold… Breathe out…

Why does everyone know what customer discovery is except me? A bit more pressing, perhaps. But not a problem that could be solved in the next few minutes before the meeting.

His mind jumped yet again, *Is Alex the right person to be leading Sales?* It was the question that had started everything. Or so he thought. The deeper he'd gotten with Helen into the sales problem, the more it'd started to seem like this entire mess pre-dated Alex.

And anyway, Jonathan was supposed to be calming his thoughts. He refocused on his breath. *Breathe in… Hold…*

Does the board think I'm the right person to be leading the company?

This question made the whole calm-breathing attempt even more difficult, because of the thought that immediately came next.

Am I?

Now this was something he definitely couldn't answer before the 2pm meeting. Jonathan turned his chair away from his desk, away from the placard with his name on it, away from his phone and computer and never-ending pile of work, and he looked out through the office windows.

Okay. Denise said we could be doing customer discovery, but the issue is not enough resources, he thought. This, at least, seemed to be a relevant distraction.

Something needs to change there.

Breathe in... Hold... Breathe out... Hold...
Breathe in... Hold... Breathe out...Hold...
Breathe in...

"Are you coming to the tradeshow meeting with Sales and Marketing?"

The question startled him, and he realized he'd finally stopped thinking. He turned around to see Denise standing in the doorway of his office.

"Yeah, sorry," Jonathan nodded, readjusting to the reality Denise had pulled him back into. He stood up from his chair and crossed his office to meet her. "Let's go."

"Did you want your phone? You left it back there on your desk."

"No, I could do without the distraction, this is an important meeting."

Denise paused and looked at Jonathan, confused.

"...Okay then," she said, and moved to catch up with him.

"Everything alright?" Denise asked him just before they entered the conference room. "Did you go to some sort of life-changing mindfulness seminar last weekend or something?"

Jonathan just laughed at that and went to find his seat in the conference room. Alex and Ethan were already seated at the table.

"Don't worry, I found him," Denise announced as she followed Jonathan into the conference room. "He was in his office *meditating.*"

"Sorry to keep you all waiting," Jonathan smiled in lieu of responding to Denise's comment. "Maria and Mark, are you with us already?"

"I'm here." Maria's voice rang out from the conference phone.

"Mark's on as well," Alex added, rather than waiting for a response from him.

"Great, I want to make sure everyone affected hears this directly from me," Jonathan started. "After a lot of thought, I have decided to cancel our booth in the tradeshow."

For a few seconds, everyone was quiet as Jonathan's announcement sunk in.

"Just like that?!" Mark chimed in. "I already booked my travel and have a bunch of meetings scheduled for that week. This won't look good, you know, with the VARs we've been courting in Europe. Pulling out last minute will raise a lot of red flags."

Jonathan sat back in his chair and paused. He looked over at Denise. She had something of a deer-in-the-headlights expression. His gaze continued traveling around the room, past Ethan—who often had a deer-in-the-headlights look—to Alex. Alex met Jonathan's eyes and nodded slightly as if to say *good call.* The small gesture made Jonathan want to let out a sigh of relief. He took a deep breath instead.

Breathe in… Breathe out…

"I know, this seems sudden, but I've had a lot of discussions over the past few weeks about the direction of the company and what we need to do to get things back on track. Sending the team to Europe for a week with an unclear value proposition and uncertain target market is not the best use of our time."

"*All* the major players in Europe will be at this conference," Mark protested. "I mean, if we're uncertain about our target market, this is the best place to get certainty. Besides, I'm sure we can make a dent in the security market if we reduce our price."

"We don't have enough resources to go after two verticals right now," Jonathan replied. "We need to refine our focus, better define our value proposition, and complete the customer research we started before Alex joined."

"That will definitely require a different focus than selling and negotiating partnerships in Europe," Alex added. "I think it's a good idea to pull out, if this is what we want to focus on."

"I can work the messaging so that pulling out of the conference won't be a big deal," Denise said. She'd abandoned her shocked expression and was leaning forward into the conversation now, determined to help problem-solve. Denise was more confident than Jonathan had seen her in months. It reminded him of when she'd first joined the team, looked at the mess of SyncAnalytix in its earlier stage, and immediately got to work.

"People do it all the time," she added.

"Well, I think we should take a vote," Mark continued, "because I think pulling out will set a bad precedent for us in the market and with VARs, not just the ones in Europe. We'll end up regretting it."

Unfortunately, and as Jonathan had just witnessed, there were multiple sides to the argument of what to do about the tradeshow, and no perfect answer. But Jonathan knew that even if he engaged in the full discussion and put it up to a vote, there would still be no easy solution. Thinking back to the advice he'd gotten from Parth, he decided the best path forward was to work out a plan with the leadership team, and not waste time arguing over the merits of pulling out of the tradeshow.

"We won't be taking a vote," Jonathan said clearly. "Like I said earlier, I've given this a lot of thought, and I know from our last few conversations that everyone on the leadership team is in agreement."

Jonathan looked over at Alex and Denise, who both nodded. Denise was grinning like she already couldn't wait for the next step in refocusing their efforts.

"So—Mark, Maria, you guys can drop off the call. I'm going to work with Alex and Denise to create a plan for the next three months that puts the focus on finding product/market fit. We'll reconvene next week when we have more clarity on that. Until then, just keep doing what you're doing."

"Alright…" Mark hesitated, "well, you know where I stand. I hope the tradeshow is back on next week, or that I at least get to keep the meetings I scheduled." His dissatisfaction was clear, even over the phone.

"We'll see," Alex replied, leaning forward towards the conference phone. "Maria, you've been quiet, anything to add before we sign off?"

"Just taking it all in," Maria admitted. "This is a big change. Let me know if there's anything I can do to help."

"We will." Alex's hand hovered over the hang-up button. "I'll follow up with you both tomorrow, alright?"

Denise let out a sigh as Alex hung-up the phone. "So, do we need Ethan for this conversation, or can he head back to his desk?"

Ethan looked like he'd walked into the wrong conference room and overheard a conversation he wasn't meant to be a part of.

"No, Ethan can go back to his research. The three of us need to spend some time figuring out how to get things back on track before we can put some of Ethan's ideas to work."

Jonathan smiled at Ethan as he hastily got up from his chair.

"Uh, so just like what Maria said, let me know what I can do to help." Ethan said looking relieved.

Ethan must have learned in the last few minutes that it was better to take Maria's approach over Mark's and roll with the new changes. He retreated back to his desk, closing the conference room door behind him.

"Okay. Where do we start?" Alex asked.

"I went and met with someone who's a product/market fit coach," Jonathan explained, "and he encouraged me to finally make some changes. The truth is, we should have shifted gears months ago."

Jonathan could sense that both Alex and Denise agreed with him on that. It made him more confident in his next proposal:

"I'd like him to come in and help us work through a new strategy—one where we end up on the same page. Does that sound like something you'd be willing to participate in?"

"Absolutely," Denise said. She'd already perked up when Jonathan mentioned a product/market fit coach. "Just tell me if there's anything I'll need to prepare for the meeting."

"It sounds like the right way to go," Alex added. "Maybe even a better use of time than the tradeshow when it comes to Sales. I wasn't going to bring it up while we were working so hard, but I've seen some companies fall apart in that pre-tradeshow crunch. I'm glad to hear you want to change directions."

Jonathan felt another boost of confidence from that, oddly enough. "I'll hash out the details with the coach, but we should be able to plan it for next week. I'll ask him to send a preliminary agenda."

"Great," Denise smiled. They all started to get up from the table. Jonathan paused before he turned to leave and added,

"I hope it's not too late for this, but needless to say both of you have full permission to focus on customer discovery now."

"Ha!" Denise laughed.

When Alex stood up, he had that relaxed, knowing sort of smile which reminded Jonathan of why he'd hired him months ago. "I'm not sure what customer discovery is but being more focused will serve our customers better in the long-run."

12
MARKET

Somehow, during what felt like the busiest month for SyncAnalytix so far, Jonathan was no longer drowning under the weight of it all. He'd made the decision to cancel the tradeshow, which could completely change the direction of the company, and he almost felt...*more* sure of the potential of SyncAnalytix than he had a few quarters ago. Looking back, the solution of just opening up the conversation about strategy with his team—let alone starting to change that strategy—seemed so obvious. He couldn't believe it had taken him this long.

Jonathan's newfound optimism was likely due to how the energy in the office had changed after he canceled the tradeshow. Everyone was less harried and more deliberate as they were planning for their new strategy, putting together information the Sales and Marketing Team had been waiting to investigate, and getting ready for their big meeting with Parth.

He had been so busy all week that by the time Jonathan walked Parth into the conference room that morning to meet Alex and Denise and start strategizing, he realized that he wasn't nervous. Normally a meeting like this would have made him worry that he didn't have all the answers. But he was mostly just excited.

"You've both heard me talk about Parth," Jonathan began, "but before we get started, I should probably explain more about why I invited him to come in and lead us through a strategy discussion for three days."

Parth shook both of their hands, smiling, and settled into a seat at the conference table.

"Over the past few weeks, I've been thinking more seriously about our strategy and how we can work better together," Jonathan said thinking back over his last conversations with Vaughn and Helen. "Reconnecting with Parth made me realize we need to have this meeting to formalize the go-to-market strategy for SyncAnalytix together as a team.

"Since this is our first time to have a specific strategy discussion as a leadership team, and things have been moving so fast, I thought it would be good to have Parth here to facilitate things." Jonathan looked over at Parth and asked, "Do you want to take it from here?"

Parth nodded back at Jonathan and effortlessly continued where he left off. "I certainly can," he replied. "Over the next three days we'll walk through a process I've used to help startups like SyncAnalytix find a path to product/market fit. A lot of the concepts come from the major pioneers in the field of lean startup, some of whose work you're probably familiar with already. By applying these concepts to this specific situation, we can really get some actionable insight into the customer's problem and how to make a solution which solves it.

"While I usually recommend a few weeks of preparation for a discussion like this, Jonathan wanted to keep things moving after the shift in focus last week built some good momentum. So, I say we just go forward with the agenda and continue to build on the excitement I can sense around here.

"Why don't we kick things off by sharing what everyone's expectations are, and what you want to accomplish by the end of these three days."

"I can go first," Denise said, eager to get her thoughts on the table. "I want us to define a path to achieving product/market fit. What are we doing, who is doing what, and what is expected of me and my department? Even if we can just come up with general answers to these questions, it would really improve the work done by the Marketing Team."

Parth took that as a cue to stand up and move to the whiteboard. He wrote 'Market / problem / product fit' at the top left corner, starting off a list. Jonathan didn't quite understand why he'd switched the order of the words when he did, but he figured he would explain later.

From what he knew about Parth, he seemed to get a kick out of building suspense during his presentations. Next, Parth wrote 'What, who, expectations.'

Market / problem / product fit

what, who, expectations

"I second that," Alex added. "I want to make sure we're all on the same page. You know, where we are and what we should be doing. It seems obvious, but you'd be surprised how many companies I've seen and even worked for where that sort of conversation never came up."

Jonathan just nodded.

"Anything to add, Jonathan?" Parth asked as he wrote 'All on same page.'

"It seems weird to say this out loud," he said, "but I just want to know that we're spending the right money on the right things at the right time." *If there's even a way to know that for sure,* Jonathan thought.

"That's not weird at all," Parth responded. He wrote *'Spend, tasks, timing'* on the board. "It's actually a good way to articulate the stress that a founder can find themselves under. These are some solid points. Anything else?"

Market / problem / product fit

What, who, expectations

All on same page

Spend, tasks, timing

"Our business is so complex, I don't know how we'll be able to cover all of this in three workdays," Alex added. "Let alone anything else, unless someone brought a time machine."

Everyone laughed at that.

"Let's get started," Jonathan proposed. "Should I summarize where we are with the product?"

"Not just yet," Parth said as he began drawing a diagram in a different section of the board. "It might help to have a visual to look at as we work through the strategy discussion. We're going to start with the market, but at its highest level. So, the total addressable market." Parth wrote *'Market'* and *'TAM'* underneath it on the board.

"Then we'll discuss the problem and the customer before we get into the product solution." Parth wrote *'Problem'*, *'Customer'*, and *'Product / Solution'* and drew circular arrows connecting each. The diagram started to come together.

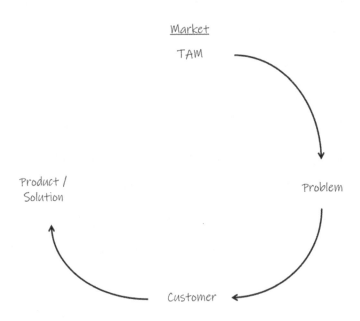

"The next time around, we'll refine the market a bit, looking at the serviceable addressable market."

Parth wrote 'SAM' under 'TAM'.

"We'll revisit the problem and customer to see if there's any further refinement needed before proposing a minimum viable product."

Parth wrote 'MVP' next to 'Product / Solution'.

"Once we have the MVP, we'll dig into what I call the minimum viable market."

Parth wrote 'MVM' under 'SAM'.

"All of that sound good?"

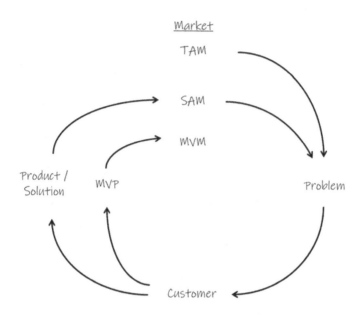

Parth took a step back to admire his drawing on the board. "This is the full process teams typically go through in weeks, not days. We're doing an accelerated version over the next few days, but it should be enough to give you the tools to continue the process and dig deeper into your strategy."

"I can see why this takes time to work through," Denise added. "There is a lot of information out there and we have only scratched the surface on most of these topics."

"Exactly," Parth said as he smiled at Denise. "We'll state some assumptions as we go through the process, but they'll need to be tested using something called 'validated learning.'"

"It looks like the flywheels I've seen used before, but not really." Jonathan paused for a moment, before asking, just to be safe: "That's not a never-ending spiral I'm looking at, is it? I mean, we'll solve our problem by the end of those loops. Right?"

Parth gave him a knowing sort of smile. "Well, I stopped drawing arrows, but that doesn't mean you're done. The next step could be to refine your focus in the existing market or expand your focus and pull more from the larger market, also called the serviceable market, or SAM."

"I sometimes feel like we go around in circles, especially in marketing," Jonathan said jokingly. "But maybe this will actually take us somewhere."

"I like to think of it as a growth spiral," Parth added.

"I hope this is the sort of process that will *build* momentum, like a flywheel, instead of a whirlpool," Denise said.

Parth nodded to Denise. "That's exactly the goal. Like the flywheel process, this is an ongoing effort that will either build momentum towards finding product/market fit or cause you to pivot in order to get things back on track."

"On that note, Denise, can you get us started with the total addressable market?" Parth asked.

"I would love to. As long as I don't have to draw anything on the board." Denise replied and smiled before flipping through her notes for the market data she'd prepared. "So, the wireless IoT sensors market is about thirty billion dollars per year growing at a thirty-two percent rate."

Parth paused as he tried to wrap his head around that number. This was a common response for people outside the IoT industry. Except the next question he asked surprised Jonathan.

"If resources were not an issue and our ability to scale was unlimited, would SyncAnalytix's product service that entire thirty-billion-dollar market? Could we achieve thirty billion in revenue?"

Jonathan wasn't the only one surprised, as it turned out. It took everyone a moment to let the question sink in. Denise replied first.

"Well...no," she said. "Major portions of the IoT market are consumer and supply chain related."

"And a lot of hardware," Alex added. "We sell analytics software to the industrial market. If we could service all those other sectors with our software, man, we'd be set for life."

"Right. So maybe a better place for us to start would be the industrial sector rather than the whole IoT market." Denise said.

"When we're talking about total addressable, it's really about the total market demand for SyncAnalytix's product specifically." Parth added. "It's common for startups to take the first big number, check the box, 'huge market', and move on. Let's dig a little deeper on this. How would you characterize the market for SyncAnalytix?"

"Like Alex just mentioned, we sell software within the industrial wireless sensor network market, and that market is about three billion dollars a year." Denise continued, "but that three billion is split across software, hardware, and services."

"We don't do hardware," Jonathan added, "but we do provide services in certain cases. Denise, do you have the split between those three sectors?"

"I'm usually reluctant to buy a market study with that level of detail, but from the searches I did—and these are all approximations—it looks like services is about 15% of the market, software is 35%, and hardware is 50%." Denise responded. She looked over at Jonathan and then Parth. "Is that what you mean by 'TAM'?"

"Full disclosure, I'm not that good at doing math in my head," Parth answered. "But I think it's safe to say that the *software* market for *industrial* sensors is around a one-billion-dollar market. There will be even more refinement when we focus in on the problem and on the segment of 'analytics' software specifically, but in the interest of time, let's start with a total addressable market of a billion dollars."

"We went from a thirty-billion-dollar market to a one-billion-dollar market, that seems like a bad way to start," Jonathan added.

Parth smiled. "It's actually a great start. You'd be surprised how many software pitch decks I've seen where the founders list the TAM as over three hundred billion, just because they sell software to enterprises. Stuff like that can lose you a lot of credibility when fundraising."

Jonathan shifted uneasily in his chair. "Sounds like we need to do a better job on our next pitch deck."

"We'll get there," Parth assured him. "When you're an early-stage startup trying to find product/market fit, the first pass through this loop is typically a shrinking exercise.

"You're all probably familiar with lean manufacturing and how it's used to improve cycle time in the production process. This is done by reducing waste, increasing value, and making continuous improvements to the process. Lean startup uses customer discovery and customer validation to reduce the time it takes to get product/market fit. To do that, we need to do very similar things: refine the focus, minimize wasted efforts, increase value to the customer, and continually get better."

"Sounds simple enough," Alex offered. "I've definitely felt like we might be wasting effort by going after too many markets."

"Yes," Denise nodded in agreement. "I've thought the same thing."

"We all have," Jonathan admitted. "Even the developers are exhausted adding feature after feature hoping it will lead to a sale.

But how do we say 'no' to a potential sale that may not be a fit when we desperately need the revenue?"

"When we are clear—" Parth paused, "specifically, as a team—when we're clear on the customers we *do* want, then it's easier to say no to the customers we *don't* want."

"Why wouldn't we want a customer?" Alex asked.

"That depends on a lot of factors," Parth began, "but the short answer is that pursuing the wrong customer creates waste."

"Before we leave the TAM discussion, quick question: who is the market leader?" Parth asked.

"Halskee," everyone answered at the same time.

"Wow," Parth responded. "Well, there you go. I guess there's no disagreement on who the leader is."

"Halskee sells mostly hardware," Denise began, "but they've been adding software and services. They are definitely the ten-ton gorilla in this market."

Jonathan described their relationship with Halskee and how it had developed over the past few months, including the most recent call that Denise participated in. As a manufacturer of IoT sensors, Halskee was always looking for opportunities to sell more sensors and had initiated the conversation with SyncAnalytix after hearing about them from a customer.

Needless to say, the thought of being acquired had come up in the back of Jonathan's mind a few times already. It wasn't what he'd imagined for SyncAnalytix at this stage, but it certainly would take some pressure off.

"It's important to know who the market leader is and their strategy, so we can define our own niche. We'll discuss more about that when we get to the minimum viable market," Parth added, "but for now, I think we have a pretty good start on the TAM. After we have a better definition of the problem, we'll want to do a bottom-up TAM as well, based on who experiences the problem and is willing to pay for a solution."

Parth looked up at the clock on the wall behind Jonathan. "We're at a good spot to break for lunch. Is everyone ready for a change of scenery?"

"Let's do it," Jonathan said as he stood up from the conference table. "I wish we were closer to your restaurant, but to keep things simple, we made reservations down the street."

"Sounds great," Parth said as the group started to move towards the door. "When we get back, we'll jump into a discussion about the *problem*."

Jonathan had wondered, when they were planning this meeting, why Parth wanted to go offsite for lunch instead of powering through their first day. Parth explained over the phone that the first day was about describing the process and building rapport. He didn't want to overwhelm everyone on day one with a data dump of completely new information.

It was an approach he'd never heard of in the startup world, let alone tried with his team. In the end Jonathan felt like he had bonded more with Alex and Denise during their lunch break than he had in the last few months of pre-meeting small talk combined.

13
PROBLEM

L unch away from the office provided a nice break from their discussion that morning, for all of them. Denise and Alex wanted to learn more about how Parth and Jonathan knew each other—which turned out to be a longer explanation than Jonathan expected. Parth shared a few startup war stories from Meranti Ventures, making everyone laugh, which reminded Jonathan of his conversation with Amir about product/market fit. He shared that anecdote, too, which brought the conversation back to the present.

Parth ran with the mention of product/market fit, even though they were on their lunch break, and casually brought up the problem statement canvas. Everyone jumped in and shared their thoughts on the topic; in order to prepare for the three-day meeting, they had all been asked to complete problem statement and business model exercises that Parth sent over email.

Each found the exercises challenging to complete on their own, with Denise being the only one who made an effort to fill out what she could and email her responses to Parth in advance of the meeting. Parth shared his belief that nailing the problem statement canvas was critical to finding product/market fit.

After lunch, Jonathan and Alex took a slight detour to check their email for any urgent issues before making their way back to the conference room. Once everyone settled in, Parth moved to an empty section of the whiteboard.

"Now that we have a better idea of the market opportunity, let's dive into the problem. More specifically," he said, "let's talk about how the customer experiences the problem."

Parth started another diagram. As he drew out the major sections, he talked through each one. Jonathan could tell he did these sorts of meetings a lot. His whiteboard handwriting was incredible.

"Like we did for the market discussion, let's review the entire process before we jump into specifics. The first thing we want to identify is the *'Context'* and the *'Problem'* that the customer has. Next, we want to estimate what their problem costs them, the *'Impact'*. This can be time, money, lost opportunities, additional resources. The more costs we can brainstorm, the better."

Context $\longrightarrow$ Problem $\longrightarrow$ Impact

Jonathan heard scribbling, and when he looked over, he saw that both Alex and Denise were copying Parth's diagrams. Denise had already started to circle different sections and add her own notes. Jonathan turned his attention back to the board.

"After discussing the cost the customer incurs due to the problem, we need to consider how they might be solving the problem now. What *'Alternatives'* exist. Some problems can't actually be solved, but some just require various workarounds and hacks. Whatever the case may be, it's crucial to understand how they currently deal with the problem. Weaknesses and shortcomings in the existing alternatives create an *'Opportunity'* for a new solution.

"Finally, we'll touch on how SyncAnalytix can solve the customer's problem, and which combination of software, services, and workflows we can provide to do so. How we create a competitive *'Advantage'*"

Alternatives → Opportunity → Advantage

"We'll conclude the problem discussion with a brief analysis of the business model; *how much* will the customer pay for the solution we provide."

Denise finished her notes, for now, and sat back in her chair. She probably had her thoughts going in all different directions, but it only seemed to motivate her. "Now it's my turn to say this is a lot to cover, but I feel like I've been waiting all year to touch on these things," she said.

Alex laughed. He was tracking with Parth, and like Denise, looked more excited than anything. That was probably a pretty good sign that they needed to be incorporating regular discussions about strategy.

"It is," Parth said as he sat down. "Understanding the customer problem is the most important thing we'll discuss."

"More important than the product?" Jonathan asked.

"Definitely," Parth responded. "In the tech space, we get so eager to design and build a product sometimes that we actually shortchange the task of understanding the problem we are trying to solve."

Parth paused to confirm that everyone was following along. "And if we don't have a deep understanding of the problem, we can't truly understand the customer."

"I have a feeling we know all this stuff already, to be honest," Jonathan confessed, "but I might have skipped over the part where we actually talk about it as a team."

"Let's jump in then, who wants to get started defining the customer problem—and the impact they experience?" Parth asked the group.

"I don't have as much technical knowledge as Jonathan about what our software does," Alex began, "but I can share what I hear from customers."

"Perfect!" Parth encouraged him to go on.

Alex leaned back in his chair, gesturing with his hands. "Really, the *best* customer calls come when someone's interested in our help analyzing data on their IoT platform. Essentially, they want to see the benefits of collecting all the data. So, maybe the problem is that their platform doesn't have enough analytics capabilities."

Jonathan and Denise both nodded at that. Jonathan hadn't realized it until now, but that had typically been the context for his best interactions with potential customers as well.

"That's great," Jonathan said.

"Yes, it's encouraging to know some of our inbound marketing efforts are working," Denise added.

"Sounds promising," Parth added. "Let's dig a little deeper into the root cause of why this is a challenge for the customer. What problem are they trying to solve with increased analytics capabilities?"

"The shift to IoT gives them access to sensors with more capabilities," Jonathan offered, "but with more capabilities comes more data. Most companies are unprepared to process all that data and lack the skill required to do anything with it. We fill that gap by providing best-in-class analytics capabilities."

Parth nodded as he thought through what Jonathan said. Finally he replied, "It's my understanding that technology advancement doesn't typically *create* customer problems, it solves them. What problem would cause a customer to shift to IoT or to seek out analytics capabilities?"

"Why can't we just go with lack of analytics capabilities as the problem?" Jonathan asked. "That's the problem we solve, and it sounds like we align with what our customers need."

Parth seemed caught off guard by Jonathan's question, or maybe by the fact that he asked another question instead of going along with the line of discussion. He paused for a moment.

"Let me see if I can offer a different perspective," Parth began as he moved to an empty section of the whiteboard. "This should give you some insights into where I was going with this, but we can definitely take a different path.

"From the customer perspective, when they have a problem that needs to be solved, they will use a five to ten step process. For simplicity, let's look at a five-step process."

Parth wrote *'Define'*, *'Root Cause'*, *'Identify'*, *'Implement'*, and *'Measure'* on the board and connected them with arrows.

Define ⟶ Root Cause ⟶ Identify ⟶ Implement ⟶ Measure

"In the define stage, the company is focused on identifying and defining the problem they need to solve. This need is typically driven by growth opportunities or cost reduction initiatives. When you are providing a solution, the bigger the problem, the better.

"Once they define the problem, they work to understand the root cause. For example, if a customer wants to reduce manufacturing costs, they need to understand what their cost drivers are.

"Once they know their root cause, then they work on identifying a solution. After identifying possible solutions, a decision is made, a solution implemented, and results measured. Does this all make sense? I'm running through it pretty quick."

Parth scanned the room and sensed everyone was ready for him to get to the point.

"If the implementation meets its measurement goals, then they're done. If not, there is a smaller five step process to try and fix the implementation issue."

Parth added a circle with a '5' inside it and two arrows to his diagram.

Jonathan looked as if he just had a huge realization.

"So, you're saying we can either be the solution to the customer's problem, or a solution to their implementation issue?"

"Yes, exactly!" Parth exclaimed. "Just to be clear, it's not the end of the world to be the solution to an implementation issue, but the bigger opportunity is always in solving the customer's initial problem. What we really want is to be the primary vendor of the solution, versus a supporting vendor. A supporting vendor provides the solution to an implementation issue."

"I think I know the answer already, so this may just be a rhetorical question," Jonathan began. "But if we're the fix to someone else's implementation, doesn't that make us more likely to get acquired or lose out in the long run? I don't think I like either of those options."

Parth nodded his head in agreement. "Not always, but those two outcomes are the most common. It depends on how big the implementation issue is and whether or not the primary vendor can solve it at some point."

Now it was time for Denise's realization. "This is what's going on with Halskee right now," she said looking at Jonathan. "Am I right?"

"Yes, and how we exited BlackBee." Jonathan answered.

"Being acquired by a strategic partner can be a great exit," Parth began as he offered a path forward. "So, we have two directions we can go here. We can define the problem in terms of the larger, primary problem, or in terms of fixing an implementation, which in this case, I believe, is their implementation of IoT software.

"Again, either way is fine, I just wanted to make sure everyone understands the difference."

The room was silent as they waited to hear how Jonathan wanted to proceed.

"I think we can do more than fix an implementation issue, and I don't want an early exit to a strategic partner," Jonathan said. "Let's look at what it takes to be the primary vendor."

Denise and Alex nodded their heads in agreement.

"Ok then, back to the previous question," Parth said, bringing the conversation full circle. "What problems are customers trying to solve with analytics capabilities or why do they shift to IOT in the first place?"

"How about this," Alex said. "A few of the customers I spoke to mentioned turnover as a source of stress. One firm even knew the statistics related to time-on-job and productivity. What I hear a lot is that operations staff are beginning to retire, all their expertise is going with them, and replacing them is hard. Loss of the intellectual capital can be a big problem."

"That's definitely true. Loss of intellectual capital is a problem for companies in general, but how does that specifically relate to the market for IoT analytics software?" Parth asked.

"Well," Denise piped up. "In older production environments, expert operations staff learned how to do proactive maintenance. The increased complexity of IoT platforms makes it more expensive and demanding to train employees on how to detect anomalies."

Parth stepped back and thought for a moment. "Loss of intellectual capital seems like a context issue and ineffective anomaly detection seems like an implementation issue."

Parth wrote *'loss of i-capital'* under the heading *'Context'*.

Context $\longrightarrow$ Problem $\longrightarrow$ Impact

loss of i-capital

"What big problem would a customer be trying to solve by implementing IoT software? Or, as it's apparently called, a 'smart factory initiative.'" Parth smiled.

Jonathan leaned forward and Denise put her pen down.

"You've done your research," she said to Parth. "And I think I see what you're getting at. I always assumed that since we aren't a full smart factory solution, we should define smaller problems. I guess I've been focused on the part we do well instead of looking at it from the customer's perspective."

"We may not have a full smart factory solution," Parth responded, "but we should be aligning with the big initiatives to solve big problems as much as we can. Think back to the five-step problem solving process, what problems are customers experiencing that they may try to solve with a smart factory initiative?"

"Things like asset efficiency, quality, and lower cost seem too generic to list as problems." Jonathan offered. "How do you go from the benefits that smart factories promise to a customer problem?"

"By working with customers to understand the context and what their goals are," Parth began. "They'll start by asking for benefits. We have to dig deeper to uncover the problem they need to solve."

"Context," Alex interrupted. "That sounds like a SWOT analysis is needed for each customer."

Parth nodded in agreement. "At least for each vertical."

"Take asset efficiency that Jonathan just mentioned," he continued, "the competitive environment or the company's current financial resources will influence how asset efficiency impacts the company. If financial resources are constrained, it might be more cost effective to increase the output of their current equipment instead of investing in new equipment. On the other hand, if competitors are investing in new equipment which doubles output, the company may be facing the problem of how to double their own production in order to stay competitive."

"If we consider just equipment efficiency from a production standpoint, we could add 'system downtime' as a problem," Jonathan said. "That has a significant impact on overall equipment efficiency."

"What might be the root cause of system downtime?" Parth asked.

Jonathan thought for a moment.

"Unscheduled maintenance is a root cause," he finally responded, "and false alarms. Both cause unnecessary system downtime."

"Oh yeah, that was the case at First Oil," Alex added. "They implemented some new sensors for 'better' performance which signaled a bunch of alarms that all turned out to be false. Totally overloaded their response team. While they were chasing down the false alarms, the operators missed a serious alert which resulted in system failure. They were cleaning up that mess for weeks."

Parth added '*unscheduled maintenance*' and '*false alarms*' on the board under '*Context*'. He then wrote '*system downtime*', '*performance*', and '*system failure*' under '*Problem*'.

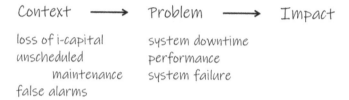

Context $\longrightarrow$ Problem $\longrightarrow$ Impact

loss of i-capital   system downtime
unscheduled   performance
      maintenance   system failure
false alarms

Jonathan wondered sometimes how Alex managed to share so many anecdotes from companies without mixing the names up.

"We'll come back to 'performance,' but for now, how does 'system downtime' compare to the implementation issue of 'ineffective anomaly detection'?" Parth asked. "Are the two related?"

Denise looked over to Jonathan who considered the question before answering.

"Better anomaly detection solves the system downtime problem by reducing false alarms and improving predictive maintenance. So, would anomaly detection be more of a solution?" Jonathan asked Parth.

"Based on what I have heard so far, it sounds like ineffective anomaly detection is an alternative shortcoming," Parth said as he pointed to where '*Alternatives*' was written on the board. "This might create an opportunity if it is a reason why customers cannot solve the problem with the current alternatives."

Parth wrote '*anomaly detection*' under '*Opportunity*'.

Alternatives → Opportunity → Advantage

anomaly detection

"You mentioned better performance," Parth said looking over to Alex. "Do you have any thoughts on what problem First Oil hoped to fix with better performance from their sensors?"

"I'm not entirely sure," Alex responded. "To be honest, they mentioned that in passing."

Alex paused as he thought for a moment. "I can say that First Oil has been working on different initiatives to increase productivity, so it could have been related to increasing production or reducing unplanned system downtime. But once I heard they were struggling with analytics, I launched into a discussion about our product. Was that bad?"

"It's better to take the time to dig as deep as you can into the customer problem," Parth responded. "The problem they are trying to solve in order to increase productivity or decrease downtime could be the same or different.

"If we make an assumption about the problem and only talk about our solution, we rely on the customer to make the connection as to whether or not our solution will solve their primary problem."

"So," Alex began, "talking to the customer about their problem is good, talking about our product before we understand their problem, not so good."

"Correct," Parth continued. "No matter where the product sits in the solution chain, we want to be able to tie it back to the primary problem the customer is trying to solve."

"So we can be more than just a fix to their broken analytics implementation?" Jonathan asked.

"I think you're starting to get the hang of this," Parth said, looking over to Jonathan. It gave Jonathan a boost of confidence.

"So, identifying more problems would be great, but we can move forward with these first few."

Denise started to say something and then changed her mind. Jonathan was going to let it slide, but he remembered that this was supposed to be the kind of meeting where *everything* was up for discussion.

"Did you want to add something?" Jonathan asked Denise.

"Well," Denise began, "I was going to add 'lack of sensor data' to the list, but I'm not sure if that should count as a customer problem."

Parth looked like he was thinking. Jonathan already had an idea of how to respond, so he went first.

"Let me see if I can walk through this," Jonathan said, looking over at Parth. Parth smiled and nodded. "Our sensor data provides an opportunity for faster machine learning, but learning is only feasible after the customer has already implemented an analytics system. So that makes lack of sensor data a problem that occurs after implementation. Do we categorize that as a customer problem or an alternative shortcoming?"

"I would say that it doesn't meet the criteria for a customer problem, but I have a feeling this will come up when we start to talk about the opportunity." Parth wrote '*sensor data*' under '*Advantage*'.

Alternatives → Opportunity → Advantage

anomaly detection   sensor data

"Customers do make decisions based on factors that reduce implementation costs or duration, but this isn't as important as solving the problem directly. Still, those factors can create a competitive advantage."

Denise added to her notes.

"To wrap-up the first part of this discussion, we've identified three customer problems: system downtime, performance, and system failures."

Parth took a step back and pointed to '*Alternatives*' on the board. "Can someone take a stab at a general answer to 'how does the customer solve the problem today?'"

Everyone started talking at once, but Denise and Alex quickly yielded the floor to Jonathan.

"I think I might get too technical on how they solve it today," Jonathan began, "and I don't want to monopolize the meeting. What are your thoughts Denise?"

"Oh, okay," Denise said. She seemed surprised at first but took the opportunity to speak her mind.

"Well, from the marketing perspective, it seems like they solve the 'system downtime' problem now with expert staff, which comes from years of working with the equipment. If you work in a plant for 20 years, you learn how to read the lights and gauges and determine what they mean and when the equipment needs to be serviced. Which, I think, to Alex's point earlier, is why companies are so concerned about losing their experienced staff."

"I agree," Alex added next, "but they have new challenges if they move to IoT and try to implement predictive maintenance."

"Why is it challenging for them?" Parth asked.

"Challenging in a sense that the experts at monitoring a system often don't think in terms that are easy to translate to programming new analytics software, or, worse, they've already left the company and taken that expert knowledge with them."

Alex paused then, deep in thought. "I can actually think of a few sales calls where the company was trying to deploy analytics using internal resources and was either..." he started counting on his fingers, "...trying to get everything implemented themselves *before* their expert retires; or their expert *already* retired, and they've just realized they have no idea what to do without expert knowledge."

"Do you ever encounter someone who is in none of those stages, maybe because they don't think it's an issue?" Parth asked.

"I'm sure they're out there," Alex responded, "but I haven't come across anyone with an IoT platform who wasn't trying to implement some form of analytics to get insights. That's usually why they call us."

"The IoT platforms are really pushing their analytics solutions," Denise added, "but they struggle with implementation. I think that has really increased awareness that there is limited availability of experts."

"So, are the IoT platform providers a competitor for you as an alternative to solve the problem?" Parth asked.

"Not really," Jonathan responded, looking over at Denise who was deep in thought. "They provide integration services, but nothing specialized enough to get to predictive algorithms and failure detection."

"That's true," Denise said. "If we think in terms of implementation issues. But, if we want to be the primary vendor like Parth described earlier, then we will need to expand the product to include more features."

Parth let her finish, and then stopped where the conversation was going before it got too technical. "Hold on a second," he said, "it sounds like we may be jumping into technical discussion about features. Jonathan, did you have anything to add to what Alex and Denise have said about current solutions?"

"I agree with everything so far," Jonathan began, "I would only add the alternative: once they make the decision to move to IoT, if they don't have internal resources, they hire a VAR and have them spend months on implementation."

"So, at a high-level, customers are *trying* to solve these problems by implementing analytics systems with VARs."

Parth wrote '*internal resources*' and '*analytics with VAR*' on the whiteboard under '*Alternatives*'.

Alternatives → Opportunity → Advantage

internal resources   anomaly detection   sensor data
analytics with VAR

"I think that's accurate," Jonathan offered.

"That's probably as deep as we want to go into a technical description of the alternatives," Parth continued. "I would encourage you to dig deeper into the problem when you meet with customers. Like we discussed over lunch, the goal is to become experts in the customer problem, its impact, and how they try to solve it. Now we want to try to estimate the impact of these problems."

"I don't know if we have that level of detail," Denise said. "We've officially surpassed the market research I'd prepared for this meeting. Alex, do you have any estimates like that?"

Alex thought for a moment. "Not off the top of my head, but it's easy enough to get while we are talking with customers. They usually know the cost if it's a big number. Sometimes they'll share those numbers without being asked."

Alex shared a few anecdotes about customer meetings when cost numbers had been discussed. None of his stories contained actual dollar amounts which would have answered Parth's question, but he kept everyone entertained for a few minutes until Parth found an opportunity to refocus the conversation.

"Depending on the context, the impact to the customer of these problems could be things like efficiency, quality, or cost. I tend to recommend a shortcut to estimate the financial impact in these situations, so we don't get stuck on analysis paralysis," Parth offered. "It works like this: what is the average annual subscription price of SyncAnalytix software?"

"Our ASP is around $50,000 per year right now and we're signing three-year deals with a $30,000 setup fee," Alex responded.

Parth smiled. "Those numbers should be easy enough to work with. Ok, so the total annualized cost of all those fees is $60,000. Let's classify problems as either low, medium, or high cost. Low cost being half the annual price, or $30,000. Medium cost is two times the annual price, or $120,000. And high cost is around ten times the annual price, or $600,000. Is everyone with me?"

"Sounds a little arbitrary to me," Jonathan said. "Is this based on some sort of analysis that a marketing think tank did?"

Parth let out a hearty laugh. "No, sorry, I don't have a research study for you to reference. Engineers love to ask that," he said. Alex laughed at that.

"I use these multiples mainly to create a wide range to work with. How much the problem *costs* says a lot about how much someone is willing to *pay*."

"I can see where this is going," Alex said. He was leaning forward, ready to talk about money. "I can tell you right now, 'system downtime' could be low cost but may go up to medium if the plant is shut down for an extended period, and 'system failure' is a medium cost problem but could be high cost in some situations, depending on what's at stake. I have no idea what a 'performance' problem costs."

"Perfect," Parth said as he wrote an '*L/M*', '*TBD*', and '*M/H*' next to the three problems on the board. "The solution that provides the most value to the customer is the one that addresses the highest cost problem. Any time spent solving the low and medium costs problems is wasted."

Context $\longrightarrow$	Problem $\longrightarrow$	Impact
loss of i-capital	system downtime	L/M
unscheduled	performance	TBD
maintenance	system failure	M/H
false alarms		

Parth looked around the room and noticed blank stares from Alex and Jonathan. Denise, on the other hand, was taking notes and nodding her head in agreement.

"Is there something about this shortcut that doesn't make sense?" Parth asked Jonathan and Alex.

"If we can solve the other problems as well, why would that time be wasted?" Jonathan asked. "Are you saying we should stay away from customers who say they have problems that cost less than $120,000? This still seems rather arbitrary to me."

Parth paused for a minute.

"*Wasted* may seem extreme, but in terms of lean startup and how we want to create the most amount of value for customers while maximizing efficiency, focus is critical. As we talk about the solution

SyncAnalytix can provide, my guess is that solving three different problems will require three different products.

"When working on finding product/market fit, it's best to focus on one problem and one solution at a time. Ideally the solution we focus on is one that we can quickly provide which solves the most expensive customer problem."

"I like the 'one problem, one solution' idea," Denise said.

"I'm on board," Alex added. "Actually, when I think about the problems we captured, they're all different layers of the same problem, which is the ultimate problem—system failure. Customers worry about intellectual capital because an untrained operator or understaffed operations department might cause someone to miss something."

"Which could lead to system downtime or a system failure," Denise continued. "And downtime or a failure…"

"Could shut down production which leads to lower throughput and increased cost," Alex finished.

Parth let out another laugh. "You guys are quite the team. Now that we're all on the same page, how far can you get right now with solving these problems? Can you prevent system failures?"

"*Prevent* might be too strong a term right now," Jonathan said, "although it'd be great if we could say that at some point with confidence. We are currently in early development on a framework that might one day actually be able to prevent system failures."

Jonathan couldn't help but wish their technology was more advanced already. If they had that sort of technology, something no one else on the market was offering, he could imagine a good amount of their sales issues magically vanishing.

Jonathan considered bringing up the product roadmap, at the very least to see what Parth would have to say, but he stopped himself. After all, that was the sort of wishful thinking which had led them to their current situation: putting the product before the customer. Based on today's discussion, he anticipated they would need to revisit the technology roadmap after meeting with customers.

"I think we're off to a good start, but I need to speak up before we get too deep into the next topic," Alex said, pushing back from the table. "I won't be of much use to anyone this late in the afternoon until I get a couple laps around the block and maybe another cup of coffee. Is it ok if we take a break before moving forward?"

"I could use a break to check my email," Jonathan added. "I want to make sure there's nothing holding up the developers."

"Me too. Well, minus the developer part," Denise said.

"Actually," Parth cut in, "I know startups like to work long hours, but I'd say we're at a good stopping point for today. We can pick things up in the morning by looking at the ideal customer profile and the product. I always recommend that teams take the rest of the day off so today's discussion has time to sink in."

Jonathan didn't argue with that; neither did anyone else. Parth was the expert on this process after all.

"Sounds like we've got a deal," Alex added. The team followed his lead and started getting up from the table.

As everyone was leaving the conference room, Denise whispered her excitement for the next day's session to Alex. "I'm curious how technical the discussion of product will be tomorrow, since Jonathan likes to get into the details, but Parth likes to keep it high-level."

Alex agreed that he was also curious.

After escorting Parth to the lobby, Jonathan made it back to the doorway of his office before pulling out his phone to check his notifications from the past few hours. When he saw the long series of messages waiting for him, he realized a cup of coffee would probably be necessary before getting caught up in the whirlwind. Then he'd be able to make it a few more hours at the office, long enough to avoid rush hour traffic on the way home.

Jonathan considered his plan for a minute and thought about what Parth had said about being 'at a good stopping point.' It may have been the first time someone had used that phrase in this office.

In the end, he put his phone back in his pocket and turned away from his office—*if I leave now, I just might be able to make dinner with Margot and the kids.*

14
CUSTOMER

The second day started with more excitement than the first. The team showed up eager to get started, and most importantly, eager to talk strategy. Alex and Parth made it to the conference room before the others and ended up in a discussion of their careers, looking for any overlap. Both of them were surprised to discover that their paths had almost crossed at least three times.

Denise and Jonathan showed up soon after 9am. Parth turned his attention to Jonathan as they walked into the room.

"Did you know Alex joined Rham Systems after Meranti led their Series C?" Parth asked him. He realized a beat later, "wait, that probably came up in the interview, didn't it."

"Yeah, we talked about that when we first connected," he answered.

Denise and Jonathan took their seats around the conference room table. Denise opened her notebook and Jonathan could tell she had been looking forward to this.

"Did you do any work with Rham Systems?" Jonathan asked Parth.

"I talked to them a few times," Parth said. "We never formally worked together, though. Rham Systems was big in the industrial space. Totally different marketing strategy than what our target customers were doing at the time, so it wasn't a good fit."

"I'll say," Alex added. "They pretty much stayed hands-on until the product was fully developed."

"Sounds like another place I know," Denise offered.

Parth took her cue and pushed away from the table. "And a great segue to our discussion this morning— customers." He made his way to the whiteboard, still full of their notes from yesterday.

"So, we started with a high-level view of the market and a discussion of the problem. For our next step we're going to build the ideal customer profile. Essentially, what type of customer not only experiences the problem in a significant way but is actively looking for a solution?"

"That's what I'm talking about," Alex said as he leaned back in his chair. "Pain that leads to purchase!"

Parth smiled and laughed to himself as he wrote a list of adjectives on the board: 'Ready', 'Willing', 'Able', and 'Made successful.'

Ready

Willing

Able

Made successful

"Alex, do you mind starting us off?" Parth asked. He turned towards the group, keeping his marker pointed to the list. "When you think about the customer, what persona would qualify as 'ready',

136

'willing', and 'able' to make a purchase decision, and can be 'made successful' by solving the problem?"

Parth paused for a moment to see if anything came to Alex's mind right away. Sensing he needed some time to think, he elaborated:

"When a customer is 'ready', that means they know they have a problem and have an urgency to solve it. Looking at the different problems we listed yesterday: 'system downtime', 'performance', and 'system failure'—who would know if they have one or more of those problems?"

"Well, all three problems would be on the radar of the engineer or plant manager," Alex began. "We get calls from both."

He was the kind of person who usually had a quick answer for everything; it was interesting for Jonathan to see him take more time to think as they worked through these brainstorming sessions with Parth.

"System failures can go a couple of levels above the plant manager, though, because of the financial impact. That being said, I think the engineer knows the problem best."

"Are they also willing to solve the problem?"

Alex twirled his pen around his index finger as he thought about Parth's last question. "Not always. System downtime can be viewed as a necessary evil.

"I'd say they're most likely to make a purchase decision if system downtime is increasing or if there's been a recent system failure. I can't see someone spending $60,000 a year for incremental improvements."

"Interesting," Parth said as he thought about the severity of the three problems. "So, the context of increasing downtime or a recent system failure is important."

Parth added both *'increasing downtime'* and *'recent failure'* to his list under *'Context.'*

Context $\longrightarrow$	Problem $\longrightarrow$	Impact
loss of i-capital	system downtime	L/M
unscheduled	performance	TBD
maintenance	system failure	M/H
false alarms		
increasing downtime		
recent failure		

"If the ideal customer is the plant engineer, do they have the authority and budget to solve their problem?"

Jonathan thought about the way the discussion had moved back and forth from customer to problem to customer. Talking about the problem had seemed to get them further in less time, but now Parth was suggesting they go backwards and talk about defining an 'ideal customer'. At first, he didn't want to interrupt, but convinced himself to speak up anyway.

"Isn't it important to pick which problem to solve before defining the ideal customer?" Jonathan asked. "I know this is all part of the process, but right now we've got a lot of evidence that our sweet spot is reducing system downtime related to false alarms."

"I'm glad you brought that up, actually." Parth pivoted his attention to Jonathan. "For our first time working through this whole spiral, the goal is to come up with as many ideas as possible, even if the best idea might seem to pop out right away."

"We are on the first pass," Parth added as he circled 'customer,' "so we are still gathering information."

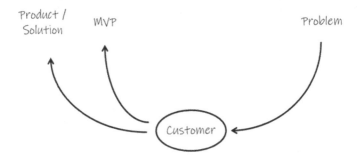

"So, we don't want to drop any 'problems' just because we don't solve them right now?" Jonathan rephrased for clarification.

"Exactly. We want to capture them all. And then we want to think strategically about which one to focus on.

"If you were to go through this process before designing the product, you can see how this would influence the development of your first release or minimum viable product. Since we already have a product, we'll want to take that into consideration when we get to the minimum viable market."

Jonathan tried to remember the initial discussions he had with customers when they were first developing the product. Without meaning to, he let his mind wander to what it would be like to design the product knowing what he knew now.

Denise must have recognized the look on his face.

"Thinking of redesigning the product already, huh?" she asked.

"You know, I think we both spend too much time here."

Denise laughed. She didn't deny it.

"The goal is a holistic view of the customers and the problems they are trying to solve," Parth offered. "If we pick one problem too early, we might miss out on learning what's most important to the market."

"Ok, I get what you're saying. Sorry to get us off track."

"Not at all," Parth assured Jonathan. Then, looking back to Alex, he picked up where they had left off. "Does the engineer have the budget and authority to purchase SyncAnalytix software?"

"Usually, no," Alex responded. "They're technical gatekeepers but they don't have the budget authority. That would be the plant manager."

"What can you tell us about the plant manager?"

"Right," Alex responded, "the plant manager. I would say in most cases the plant manager has the budget to purchase SyncAnalytix, at least at our current pricing. We could probably double our price before losing approval authority at the plant manager level."

"Great, so that means plant managers are ready, willing, *and* able," Parth said, "Of course the last thing we need to determine is if they can be made successful by solving their problem."

Alex nodded slowly. "Let me think. From the limited discussions I've had just with plant managers, it definitely depends." he answered. "If they report certain metrics up the management chain, then yes, using our product can improve .those metrics and make them more successful."

"On the other hand," Denise added, "if they run their own operation, then reducing system downtime could just be one of many initiatives not reported up the management chain."

"Or," Jonathan interjected, "fixing a throughput issue in one area uncovers a constraint in another."

"You'll definitely want to make this question a part of your discovery process," Parth began, "and pay attention to whether the manager you're talking to is reporting system downtime, false alarms, and other metrics to their senior management. Whenever possible, ask them how they report performance and measure success."

"And if they understand the theory of constraints," Jonathan added.

"Noted," Denise said, at the same time she wrote the suggestions down in her notes. "That's a good way to refine who we prioritize as potential customers."

Jonathan slowly shook his head from side-to-side as he thought about the fact that they'd have way more success if they turned their ideal customer into a potential customer, and not the other way around. He could feel himself smiling.

Parth nodded and wrapped up the discussion to that point. "Okay, as a first pass, the plant manager seems to meet the criteria for our ideal customer. When you get out and start talking to plant managers, you'll want to validate these points. There will probably be slight differences depending on the industry, the company they work for, and the size of the plant."

"Definitely," Alex said. "I don't think I've ever had two customers that were in the exact same situation

Alex provided a few customer stories that explained the many different situations a plant manager might be in. Just like he mentioned, each story was unique, and unsurprisingly, several of them included anecdotes that made the rest of the room laugh. He summed up by saying that it was fun just talking with customers, but that having items to validate would enable him to move the discussion closer to a sale in the right situations.

"I can tell you already that an increased level of customer insights will make a huge difference," Denise added. "Personas can be so complicated that we haven't had the time to create any."

"And then we waste a lot of time talking to anyone who will listen." Alex added, thinking back to Mark's approach for finding new opportunities. "For example, going after the security market seems like a huge distraction and not worth the time and effort. Having a single target market keeps things simpler for my team."

"I like to keep things simple," Parth added with a smile. "I would rather focus just on conversations as the starting point. If Sales and Marketing work together, you can begin filling out more details, like hashing out the economic versus technical buyer, the buying process, and your channels. Most important, though, is the 'who' and 'why,' and I think we have a great start on that."

"Seems simple enough to me," Jonathan added, "but I'll admit I've been a little disconnected from the process since we brought on Alex."

"Really?" Parth asked. He looked surprised, which made Jonathan worry that taking a step back from sales was not the right decision. "You'll definitely want to reconnect. In fact, the three of you need to work together during customer discovery and customer validation. The more you can articulate and test each other's assumptions, the better."

"I can see what you mean," Denise added. "I remember feeling like I understood the customer a lot better when it was just me and Jonathan working to make sales. Back when there was less focus on functional roles."

Parth was nodding while Denise spoke.

"Building functional departments before product/market fit can lead to the wrong behavior; I've seen it happen before." he said. "When you go from a customer-focused core team to functional departments too early, it's referred to as premature scaling. But we might be getting off track. I think we have enough time to get through one more exercise before we break for lunch. It's called a day-in-the-life of your customer."

"Is there a diagram involved?" Alex asked. "Because each time you draw a diagram on the board, it leads to a two-hour discussion. Which would have us skipping lunch altogether, I think."

Parth laughed. "No diagram this time."

Jonathan let out a sigh of relief, which only prolonged the laughter in the room.

Parth smiled as the laughter died down and then began describing the next exercise.

"The day-in-the-life is about describing the context to better understand the problem your customer experiences, how they experience it, and what their current alternatives are for solving it. This exercise helps you polish your understanding of the problem and the customer. We'll talk about the 'before' context, meaning, what life is like *before* the customer has a solution to their problem.

"You'll want to work through each of the problems and create a day-in-the-life brief, which you can…?" Parth directed his question towards Alex.

"Confirm with customers," Alex responded with a smile.

"Exactly," Parth continued. "Let's start with 'false alarms' that lead to 'system downtime.' I'm not sure who knows this, so feel free to answer if you have some thoughts. What is the situation when the plant manager experiences a 'false alarm'?"

"False alarms can happen at any time, so I'm not sure if I could define just one situation," Alex replied first.

"Right," Denise added. "Are you talking about the time before a false alarm, or once they realize that there's been a false alarm?"

"It could be either," Parth responded. "Which one has more impact on the customer?"

Parth stood up and went to the board. "I promise not to draw a diagram, but it might help to see what other items we'll address when we're talking about a day in the life."

On the board, Parth wrote the list: '*Situation*,' '*Desired outcome*,' '*Attempted approach*,' '*Interfering factors*,' and '*Economic consequences*.'

Situation

Desired outcome

Attempted approach

Interfering factors

Economic consequences

"I'm not the expert," Parth continued, "but based on our discussions and my own thoughts about 'false alarms,' I'll walk through these different steps. So, let's say the 'situation' is that the system is shut down while they waste a bunch of time tracking down a false alarm. The 'desired outcome' is to eliminate such false alarms. The 'attempted approach' is, say, to install an IoT monitoring platform and train operators on what is a real alarm versus a false alarm. But the 'interfering factors' to this approach…"

Parth paused, the end of his marker hovering over '*Interfering Factors*' on the board.

"Okay, I'm stuck here. The 'interfering factors' in this situation would basically be the explanation for why the attempted approach is not working. Any ideas?"

"I can add something," Jonathan volunteered. "They could try to solve the problem with added training, but training isn't always sufficient because there are so many factors that cause false alarms. It could be the gradual degradation of a sensor, the interaction of two sensors, or a sensor failure, and not all of those can be caught in time. The training overhead for every possible scenario is too much. I think a plant engineer would realize that, too."

"That's what I've heard," Alex added. "A lot of people tell me that after a certain point they're just resigned to having to deal with a certain level of false alarms, especially when dealing with poor anomaly detection algorithms."

"An alternative weakness definitely counts as an interfering factor," Parth said. "As far as the 'economic consequence' goes, would a plant manager consider it wasted resources to confirm whether or not there is a false alarm?"

"Yes," both Jonathan and Alex answered, nearly in unison.

Alex spoke first. "They must send someone to check the alarm which is a waste of time and money already. Sometimes they have to shut down the plant in order to address the alarm."

"If it turns out to be a sensor issue, the shutdown can extend while they wait for new parts to arrive. Or they run without a sensor and risk a more serious failure," Jonathan added.

"So, the economic consequence of system downtime can be costly, is that what I'm hearing?"

"Very costly," Jonathan told Parth. "In fact, false alarms also include 'no alarms,' because sensor failure could also lead to no alarm, which is why we constantly capture data from the sensors. We can also track sensor degradation, false positives, and other system issues that lead to false alarms."

Jonathan noticed that everyone was looking at him intently. "Sorry, was I getting too technical back there?"

"I don't think so," Denise offered. "This is great stuff. I wish you would spend more time sharing all you know in this space. This info, especially in the context of solving the customer problem, is marketing gold. We can use it to really streamline our messaging."

"We don't want to fall into the trap of thinking that the solution is more important than the customer's problem," Parth cautioned.

"The point of this exercise is to get you thinking about the customer experience, so when you do your discovery meetings you talk more about their situation and less about your product. I encourage you to become great at asking about the customer's past experience, what they have tried to solve their problem, and what is the impact when they are unable to find a solution."

Alex and Denise nodded in agreement.

"Well, you guys nailed that exercise, I have to say," Parth offered, looking satisfied with their work. Jonathan felt it, too, and they were only halfway through the process, apparently. "Let's head to lunch and talk more about how the three of you can continue to drive the product/market fit efforts."

"Works for me," Alex said as he got up from his chair.

Jonathan and Denise stood and began to head for the door. As the four of them walked to lunch on their second day together, still keeping up their conversation, Jonathan wondered why they didn't meet more often to talk about strategy and other management topics. It was usually just quick updates regarding forecasts and tactics. He could already tell that these meetings alone were going to make a big difference.

15
PRODUCT

Alex caught Jonathan on the way back to the conference room. The two of them were already running a little late. When they finished lunch, they agreed to reconvene in fifteen minutes; Jonathan had made a few calls to check in with his team and lost track of time. Alex was apparently guilty of the same thing.

When they made it back inside, Parth and Denise were deep in conversation. Denise spotted Jonathan after he closed the door and smiled.

"I guess your fifteen-minute timer is a little off," she joked.

"Sorry," he said as he sat down. "Ended up getting pulled into a discussion with the developers about normalization."

Parth didn't seem to mind the delay. "Is that a 'normal' occurrence?" he asked with a smile.

"Only at this office!" Alex joked.

Jonathan started to answer but Denise beat him to it.

"Yeah, that's pretty 'normal' around here," Denise began in response to Parth's question. "Let's not get him started talking about relational database design, we won't get out of here before midnight."

Alex laughed as he took his seat at the conference table.

"Good call, Denise," Parth responded. "We don't want to get into any of the technical details around the product. Not today, at least."

"How can we talk about the 'product/solution' step in your diagram without discussing the product?" Jonathan asked. He watched as Alex and Denise took their notes back out, and realized he forgot, again, to bring a pen and paper to the conference room.

"I'm glad you asked." Parth stood up to return to the whiteboard.

"What is all too common," he continued, "and based on Denise's good-natured comment just now, I think is also an issue at SyncAnalytix, is a focus on the solution space and not the problem space."

Parth underlined '*Advantage*' and wrote '*own the problem space.*'

"Once we understand the customer problem, how they are impacted by this problem, how they try to solve it, and any other important market signals, we can define a solution that addresses the root cause and truly solves the problem," he explained.

"Hold on, can we talk about the difference between the solution space and the problem space?" Alex asked. "I've never used the term 'problem space' in conversations like this, but if I did it would probably be interchangeable with 'solution space'. I've got a feeling you don't see it that way."

Parth smiled. "You're right; I don't."

"You're not the only one who's unsure about the difference," Denise added.

Parth took the floor from there.

"I like to think of it in terms of being *reactive* versus *proactive*," he explained. "Reactive product design is led by feature requests. You meet with customers *after* you design the product, the customer asks for additional features, so you add features to the product in hopes of making the sale, but you may not actually be solving their problem. Prioritizing the product is a focus on the solution space. I have also heard this referred to as 'technology push.'

"With proactive product design, on the other hand, you meet with customers *before* designing the product, reach an agreement on the problem they experience and how it impacts their business, and then you design a product that solves their problem. Prioritizing the problem is a focus on the problem space. You might have heard this referred to as 'market pull.'"

"Now that I think about it, I've actually been in both situations with potential customers," Alex added, "and I can say without a doubt that proactive product design makes for a much easier sales process. I never like leading with the pitch and then feeling like I'm trying to shoehorn it back into whatever they say next."

"If you show a product idea to a customer out-of-context," Parth offered, "they will most likely give you feature feedback. Proactive product design is based on root-cause analysis. To do root-cause analysis, you need to become an expert at understanding the customer's problem."

"Okay, I feel like I should reiterate that we have a product already," Jonathan added, a little frustrated. "I don't see how changing our approach to product design is worth our time when the product already exists, and we know more than the customer about what we can do with it."

"Well, bear with me. And I may be out of line here," Parth said. He held his hands up for emphasis, and Jonathan knew he should try not to take his next words personally. "But based on our initial discussion, it sounds to me like we have a product looking for a problem to solve. To find product/market fit, we need to be proactive and create market pull."

"I think there's truth to that," Denise added, trying to defuse the tension in the air. "And I don't think Parth is suggesting that we change the product itself at this point, just improve how we market and sell it."

"I know I could use help on the Sales side of things," Alex said, "and we both know that Denise is under-staffed on the Marketing side."

"And," Denise continued, "the challenge has been getting the technical information out of your head and in front of customers in a way that makes sense to them."

Parth was nodding through both of their contributions. He looked at Jonathan with an open sort of expression, like he'd be happy to continue explaining his perspective if Jonathan was still unsure. But Jonathan felt like he was starting to understand what he'd meant in the beginning.

"Okay, I think I see what you were suggesting. I just jumped to conclusions when 'product design' came up. It sounded like we were heading back to square one."

"If all you had when we met for lunch the other day was an *idea* for a product," Parth said, "then I might propose more problem research and less go-to-market strategy. Even though you already have a product, you still need the customer research and market knowledge to inform your strategy going forward.

"When we 'own the problem space,' marketing and sales will flow from that point. Then we'll be on our way to finding 'product/market fit,' or 'crossing the chasm,' or any of those buzzwords you hear thrown around in the lean startup and venture capital space.

"The problem space can also be thought of as a market defined around the customer's problem, or an intersection of the problem and the serviceable available market.

"We talked earlier about being in the industrial IoT market, right?" Parth asked Denise.

"Yes," Denise responded. "In the analytics software segment of the industrial IoT market."

"While it's good to know that a market of some form already exists, that sounds like a solution space name. We want to define it even tighter, if we can, in order to capture some of the concepts around the problem. In fact, when you're a startup introducing a new and innovative product, it's best to focus on a small segment where such a solution doesn't exist at all, or where there is no clear market leader."

"How small does that segment need to be?" Alex asked.

"Yesterday we talked about the TAM, and, since we already have a product, we'll jump ahead and talk about the minimum viable market." Parth circled 'MVM' in his diagram.

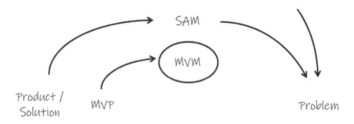

"Now, the served available market is made up of multiple, smaller markets, that I refer to as minimum viable markets. When we are looking for product/market fit, the focus should be on one small, manageable market at a time.

"There are two ways we can define the size of the minimum viable market. I prefer to start with identifying a subset of customers from the SAM who have a compelling reason to buy, but the other option is to work backward based on a revenue target. We will work through both options, but I'll let you decide where to start."

"Since we have a revenue target, let's start there," Jonathan offered.

"Great. What is this year's revenue target, Alex?" Parth asked.

"Our target for this year is three million dollars. At this point we've closed 300 thousand over seven months." Alex paused to see if Jonathan had anything to add. "We have a pretty good funnel, but deals are pushing out as they typically do in early markets."

Parth nodded at that, rather than commiserating with them on their lackluster sales this year. Parth's lack of response was reassuring to Jonathan. "Let's work with the three-million-dollar number. Of the current deals, what percent would you say fit the customer profile we've been discussing today?"

Alex rested his chin on his hand. "If I were to guess, I would say 40 percent."

"Interesting," Parth said, nodding in thought. "That's lower than I would have thought. After an exercise like what we worked through, I usually see numbers in the 70 to 80 percent range. Let's estimate that after refining the target market and the marketing message, that percentage jumps to 70 percent."

"Do you think that big of a jump is possible?" Denise asked.

"Definitely," Parth replied. He seemed so sure of it that Jonathan couldn't bring himself to doubt that answer.

"The goal of defining a minimum viable market is to set our target on a segment where we can achieve 50 percent market share in 12 months."

Parth continued, "with an annual revenue target of three million dollars, at 70 percent of our total customers coming from our target market, that would be 2.1 million in revenue. If 2.1 million was 50 percent of the market, then the market size would be 4.2 million."

"That doesn't make any sense," Jonathan began. "I can't tell investors we are going after a four-million-dollar market."

Parth smiled, "yeah, that type of pitch wouldn't have gone far at Meranti Ventures, huh?"

Jonathan shook his head 'no.'

"I agree, no CEO in their right mind would say 'we're going after a four-million-dollar market' when raising capital. Unfortunately, investor pressure to go after large markets has caused entrepreneurs to try to scale before they're ready.

"We often overlook the benefit of targeting specific market segments or verticals—this is being *focused*. Without a segment-based go-to-market strategy, we are going after the broad market and competing against market leaders: large multinational companies with more resources and the support of technical buyers."

Parth recalled a customer Alex had mentioned previously.

"When you are talking to the technical buyer at, for example, First Oil, and their choice is to go with your solution, from a startup with less than one million in revenue, or a multinational 'brand name' with billions in revenue, who do you think they will choose?"

"They'll pick the brand name," Jonathan said, clearly discouraged. "Are you saying we should just give up because it's impossible to compete with Halskee?"

"No, but I'm saying that we need to be clear and deliberate about what we're going after. Trying to be everything to everyone as an early-stage startup is the fastest path I know to failure. And trying to sell to the technical buyer when you are not the market leader is the second fastest."

"Sounds like we've been on the fast track to failure," Denise said.

"Sorry, I don't mean to be a downer," Parth admitted to her, "but, if this stuff was easy, then every startup would be successful, and failures due to 'no market need' would be rare. You guys are smart and can figure this out, just stay with me a little longer."

"I'm with you, Denise. I'm hoping there's a light at the end of this tunnel," Alex added.

Jonathan sensed both Denise and Alex were growing discouraged around trying to achieve quota—a goal he'd set with very little thought. He had an unexpected urge to rally the team.

"I see a light," Jonathan said next. "We've made some great progress so far. Yes, we've heard some things that were hard to hear, but everything Parth has said makes sense and will make us better. I still think we have a great opportunity and the right team to get things back on track."

When Jonathan finished speaking, he realized that both Alex and Denise were staring at him, almost like they were confused. He wondered for a second if he'd said something wrong.

"What?"

"Nothing," Denise said first, "I'm just a little surprised to hear you be so encouraging for once."
She immediately recoiled. "Sorry, that sounded harsh."

"Harsh, but true," Jonathan said, "I guess that's another area for improvement."

Parth waited to see if anything else needed to be said before he continued.

"Ok, so the top-down market is 4.2 million dollars. Let's look at the bottom-up approach to defining the minimum viable market. Assuming the software is $60,000, we are looking for a market which has about 70 customers."

Looking over at Denise, Parth asked, "based on the problem and customer discussion, can you think of a market segment that has 70 potential customers who desperately need a solution?"

"I'm not sure I follow," Denise responded. "Am I picking specific customers, geography, or something else?"

"Great question. I don't think I was very clear when I asked for a market segment," Parth apologized. "Ideally, this is a market that someone else has already defined, and one where the participants interact with each other. The goal is to use this first market segment as a reference point for entering the next segment. This will establish credibility with future customers."

"I can't think of one off-hand. Seventy customers might be a little small for an officially defined market."

"If we're using existing customers as a reference point for future customers, wouldn't it make sense to look at our existing customers and try to define a market around them?" Alex offered.

"Yes," Parth answered, turning his attention to Alex. "That's another method and it would make sense based on where you are— since you already have customers. Of the ideal customers that you have now, can you identify some characteristics that can build up to a market of around 70 companies?"

"Two great customers that come to mind are both oil companies," Alex began, "and they both have the same dashboard vendor. Are there other similarities that you can think of Jonathan?"

"We can certainly look into the data and see what other similarities there are. Does it make sense to go to that level of detail?" Jonathan asked Parth.

"Only if you can use it to build a market segment," Parth responded. "But you're right, getting too far into the weeds will give you information that would be hard to translate into a market segment. We're looking for similarities across our problem hypotheses that we can address to create credibility for us as a solution. What alternatives they may have tried is just one data point."

"So, the idea is that we could say 'we have 50 percent of the customers in the market we defined,'" Denise said. "I think I'm beginning to follow you on this. The 'minimum viable market' builds our credibility and collateral so we can grow to the next level."

"I don't think I could have said it better." Parth smiled. "It looks like this is all starting to come together."

"Except that in those two customer engagements, aren't we a supporting vendor?" Denise asked Jonathan. "From yesterday's discussion, I thought we wanted to move to being a primary vendor."

"I think that's right," Jonathan agreed. "I'm still trying to wrap my head around the whole primary versus supporting vendor. Parth, how do we make the transition to being a primary vendor when we don't have a full product solution?"

"That's a big part of the go-to-market strategy for lean startups," Parth began, "because most begin with an MVP which is not a full product solution. One thing that's great about early adopters is that they will engage with you before you have the full solution. They will buy your product and work with you to create a full solution to their problem.

"The worst thing that could happen is you think your product is ready for the majority market because you've done a few pilots or closed a few sales. You think it's time to scale, but actually you've been *fooled by early adopters*."

Jonathan's heart dropped into his stomach as everything finally clicked. This is exactly what had happened to them. This is why they ended up in a 'death spiral.'

But at the same time, he felt that naming their mistake was perhaps the most beneficial thing they could do. And with Parth's guidance, he felt strongly that they would be able to find a way out.

Alex looked around the room before asking "Alright, I know I should know them, but these conversations are making me doubt my own definitions. Can you give us your explanation on what early adopters and majority markets are?"

"I'm with Alex," Jonathan added. "I could use a better definition."

"Of course. I'm glad you asked." Parth made his way to an empty section of the whiteboard. "The technology adoption life cycle went mainstream with the book *Crossing the Chasm*. I won't get deep into the theory, but essentially, the adoption of an innovation has been shown to follow a normal, bell-shaped curve."

Parth drew a curve on the board and labeled two sections '*Early*' and '*Majority*'.

"The early adopters are on the left side of the chart, and the main street market, or the majority, is the large portion in the center."

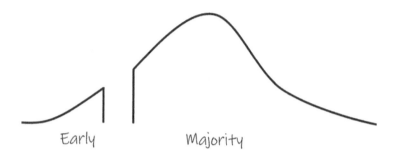

Early   Majority

"The gap is what Geoffrey Moore called the 'chasm.' His theory was that startups who failed to cross the chasm from early adopters to the majority would not succeed. His advice on how to cross the chasm became the basis for a lot of successful go-to-market strategies in the late 90s and early 2000s."

"I've seen this before," Denise said. "Is it safe to say we're stuck in that gap right now?"

"Probably," Parth nodded.

"It certainly *feels* like we're stuck," Jonathan said.

"So, to your question about how to transition to being the primary vendor," Parth said to Jonathan, "you follow the chasm crossing strategy of working with early adopters.

"Which is another reason why you want to focus on a small market. Working with early adopters to build out a full product solution is difficult and time-consuming. It's all-hands-on-deck and requires significant focus. But, when done right, it makes it easier to enter adjacent markets and continue building market share.

"Does that address your question?"

"I think so," Jonathan responded.

Parth surveyed the room to see if anyone had additional thoughts or questions. He noticed the time on the clock and was about to propose they end for the day, but then Jonathan spoke up.

"The early adopter stuff makes sense, but I'm still struggling with why we would want to limit our market to 70 customers. It just seems like we'd be selling ourselves short."

"It does seem counterintuitive, doesn't it?" Parth asked. "I like to think of it as refining the focus in order to find product/market fit. Without focus, you'll try to be everything to everyone. Your product will become feature rich and problem-solving poor."

Jonathan thought about the recent increase in feature requests that were needed to close sales. He expected Denise to comment on the 'feature rich' statement—maybe with too many recent examples—but was relieved that Parth was able to continue uninterrupted.

"We'll talk in more detail tomorrow about finding product/market fit from this point forward. And I'll tell you right now—it's a lot of work. Without a high degree of focus on a minimum viable market, you cannot own the problem space. Those companies that *do* own the problem space can find product/market fit and eventually own the market."

"So, to clarify," Denise interjected, "when we are out doing customer discovery, we're looking for early adopters who are willing to work with us on creating a full solution?"

"I was wondering that as well," Alex added.

"Yes," Parth answered. "In addition to validating our assumptions and understanding of everything else we've discussed, we should be looking for alignment with early adopters. It'll likely be 10 to 15 percent of the people we talk to."

Parth made a few quick notes on the board.

"I don't want to complicate things further because it is getting late, but startups tend to go through two phases on the way to product/market fit. The first phase is what I call product/market 'Match.' This is where we match the alternatives. Some people call this 'table stakes.'"

Match ⟶ Alignment ⟶ Fit

"The next stage is '*Alignment.*' This is where our solution, what we do as a company, is aligned with the problem the customer is trying to solve. When we find alignment, we want to close those customers if possible. Early adopters are more likely to take a risk, so those are likely the deals we'll be able to close.

"The final phase is '*Fit.*' That is when our solution is a 10x or greater improvement, the market rallies around our product, and we are taking orders faster than we can fulfill them. Geoffrey Moore referred to this phase as being 'inside the tornado.'

"Match is where most companies struggle, get stuck and eventually shut down. Alignment is a great place to be and can lead to a lot of success. Fit is the ultimate goal, but not everyone gets there, nor does everyone need to."

"Okay," Jonathan surrendered. "We've officially reached my limit on marketing theory in one meeting. Hopefully it'll all come together tomorrow."

"I can guarantee that," Parth stated. "We've run pretty late this time, so let's break here for the day. We made great progress.

Tomorrow, we'll pull it all together and map out a rough plan for customer discovery and validation."

"I'm looking forward to it. Back here at 9am sharp?" Denise asked.

Everyone agreed, and Alex and Denise made their way out of the conference room. Jonathan lingered behind so that he could walk out with Parth.

"Am I missing something?" Jonathan asked as they made their way to the front lobby. "I get the feeling that this should all be making sense to me, especially after spending two days on it. But I'm still struggling to see a clear path forward."

"You're not missing anything," Parth responded. "In fact, you're sharing concerns that most entrepreneurs and CEOs have. This lean startup stuff is different and requires new ways of thinking. The clear path forward will come as you start meeting with customers and understand the gap between your product and solving the customer's problem."

Parth paused as if he had another thought come up suddenly.

"You know, I've had this strategy discussion with executive teams in one form or another over a hundred times, and I always end up wondering how I can make things go more smoothly: *Maybe if I presented that concept differently...* or *Maybe if I added this detail here...* But the truth is, this stuff is hard. And it's different from what people learn in school."

"That's definitely true."

"Once you and your team have the tools, you'll be able to start using them and then things will make more and more sense. It's a process and it takes practice, but you guys are smart, and I have a good feeling that this will all come together."

"I hope you're right," Jonathan said, clearly exhausted after the second full day. "We might need some sort of miracle to get back on track."

"Not a miracle." Parth smiled. "You just need a process. Which is one of the things we'll focus on tomorrow."

Parth shook Jonathan's hand and gave him a pat on the shoulder. "See you then, 9am sharp."

"9am sharp."

Jonathan took a slight detour on the way back to his office to see if any customer support engineers were still in. Turning the corner, he noticed Denise had the same idea and was already in discussion with one of them about customer characteristics.

Jonathan smiled as he walked by. *Maybe I don't need to be doing everything after all,* he thought as he continued walking past his office and headed home.

16
DISCOVERY

Jonathan spent most of his commute to the office the next morning wondering where the conversation was headed next. After two days of talking through problems and customers with Parth, he figured it was time to talk about product/market fit. Or at least, he hoped that was up next—it meant they'd finally be putting all the pieces together.

Parth had arrived early and had drawn a new diagram on the board.

As everyone settled in, he began by providing an overview of what they would cover during their last day together. Again, it sounded like more than they had time to cover, and Jonathan *already* felt like they'd gone through enough discussion topics to fill a semester at Ethan's MBA program.

"We've spent the past two days discussing the market, problem, customer, and product strategy. Today is going to pull it all together, and we're going to talk about finding product/market fit."

Jonathan was relieved, excited, and, in the back of his mind, a little concerned that this would turn out to be another mind-bending conversation that made him doubt everything he knew.

"So…the elusive product/market fit," Alex said as he shifted in his chair. Finally, he leaned back, crossing his arms behind his head.

"Isn't that just what you call it when you hit sales targets and have happy customers?"

"Or high growth and a low churn rate?" Denise added.

Jonathan wasn't even sure if he had a clear enough idea in his head of product/market fit to chime in with his own definition. At least not in one sentence.

"It can be," Parth responded, "but those definitions tend to lack an actual strategy and instead just hope for the best. Some companies get lucky, but most fail because they didn't do the work to test, learn, and adapt. What we want to do today is define the steps to get there instead of just crossing our fingers and hoping we hit our sales target.

"Product/market fit starts with customer discovery, which is about defining the problem, finding out who has the problem, and determining whether or not solving the problem is important to them."

"That's probably the part I've been the most curious about," Jonathan interjected. "Customer discovery, I mean. Apparently, we're not doing it right, or maybe not doing it at all."

Denise turned to Jonathan. "I would say we've been doing at least some work in customer discovery, especially back when you and I were meeting with customers ourselves, before we brought in Sales."

"That's usually the case at most startups," Parth said. "Let me walk you through this diagram and you'll see why founders need to be involved in customer discovery from beginning to end.

"The process begins with our hypotheses about the problem and the customer. We need to take the discussion from the past few days about the problem *outside* of this conference room and to the customer."

Parth pointed to the left side of the diagram as he continued his description.

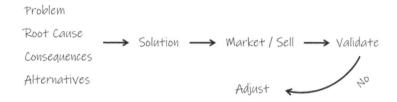

"A good goal is to talk to more than ten customers a week during discovery, in order to confirm what we believe about the *'Problem,'* the *'Root Cause'* of the problem, what *'Consequences'* they experience because of the problem, and what *'Alternatives'* they have tried to solve the problem."

Before Parth finished his last sentence, Denise spoke up.

"What if we already have a solution?" Denise asked.

"*Ten* customers a week?" Jonathan asked, clearly still stuck on Parth's opening comment.

Parth smiled. "Let's start with Jonathan's question and then address the existing solution part. Ten customers might seem like a lot if you are thinking in terms of ideal customers, like the plant manager we defined yesterday. But during discovery, we want to talk to anyone remotely related to the problem, not just who we think might be the ideal customer."

"Why would we waste time talking to someone who isn't the ideal customer?" Jonathan asked. He figured that Denise might be wondering the same thing. Although she looked more thoughtful than confused.

"Great question," Parth began. "The main part of discovery is validating what you believe with actual customers. Right now, the ideal customer profile is really just a hypothesis. We do believe that this customer exists, but that belief hasn't been tested.

"Yesterday we settled on the plant manager as the ideal customer, but if we only talk to the plant manager, we'll get one side of the story. If we talk to someone above or below the plant manager, for example, the plant engineer, and they point us to the plant manager as the decision maker, we shouldn't see it as time wasted so much as time spent validating that the plant manager is our ideal customer."

"I get it." Alex nodded. "That helps me frame any objections I might get from whomever we are talking to."

"And understand the different roles within the buying process," Denise added.

"Right," Parth said. "We're trying to build a holistic view of the customer."

"So, these discovery meetings aren't sales meetings," Jonathan concluded.

"Well, yes and no," Parth continued. "This is a great segue to Denise's question. When you are meeting with potential customers, you want to get their perspective on their problem and what they think a solution to their problem could be. This enables us to learn about how critical the problem is as well as whether or not they have an alternative solution."

"And to clarify, when I say *you*, I mean more than just Alex," he said, looking at Jonathan and Denise. "I think everyone who *can* participate in these meetings *should*. The meeting can be led by anyone, but whoever is leading the meeting should be ready and able to close a sale."

"So, if we have a solution, we should be ready to close a sale, correct?" Denise asked.

"Yes," Parth said as he shifted his focus to the *'Market / Sell'* section of the diagram. "With a caveat around alignment: if you have a solution and it aligns with the customer's perception of the solution they need, then sell it!" Parth circled the word '*Sell.*' "What have we got to lose?"

Jonathan knew that was a rhetorical question, but he couldn't help but answer such questions in his head. Even in this case, he could think of a couple things they had to lose—after all, those early, easy sales were apparently what had misled them in the first place.

Still, he sat back and focused on what Parth said next.

"The disconnect between expanding the Sales team and selling the product can be a major point of confusion in the lean startup model. Founders think, *'I have an MVP, it's time for me to hire Sales.'* Actually, when you have an MVP or a product, it's time to sell it— and if the founders are not closers, meaning they don't know how to ask for a sale, *then* you hire someone who can do that."

Jonathan could tell Parth was passionate about the last point. "So that's why you say there needs to be a closer in the meeting? Even if the purpose of the meeting isn't to make a sale?"

"Exactly, because if we get to this point in the meeting where we can make a sale, we need to make it." Parth gestured through the different steps of the diagram. "When you have alignment on the 'problem,' alignment on the 'root cause,' and alignment on the 'solution,' then close the sale.

"Don't put things off by scheduling another meeting or saying, 'we'll get back to you.' *That* would be time wasted. The ultimate way to validate our product hypothesis is to have paying customers using the product to solve their problem."

"And if we don't have full alignment?" Alex asked.

"In that case, we stay in discovery mode. We ask deeper questions in the areas where we don't have alignment. This will give us specific details about where some of our hypotheses might be wrong."

Alex was nodding while Parth spoke. He looked deep in thought.

"Anything else you want to add Alex?" Jonathan asked.

"Just taking it all in," he said. "It's a different perspective than what we've been operating under."

"In what way?"

"When we go into a customer meeting, we're only looking for alignment to make that sale. If it looks like we won't be able to close, the conversation is over."

Parth nodded. "That's a pretty common approach."

"Is that something we can change?" Jonathan asked. "I mean, if we agree that we should be doing customer discovery, then we need the Sales Team to be taking a different approach."

"That's just it," Alex replied. "We have a quota-driven Sales Team. As long as there's a quota, the account executives are going to be focused on the sale, not on discovery."

Alex let out a sigh before adding, "We should probably talk about it later, but if we switch to this approach, I definitely see an issue with how the team is incentivized.

"But we can talk about that later," Alex repeated.

"Agreed," Jonathan nodded in response. "Let's get clear on the strategy and then look at how our existing resources fit what needs to be done."

Alex directed his attention back to Parth and asked, "what about the case where we don't have full alignment, but we can make a sale?"

"It's risky," Parth began. "You must seriously think about why a customer is wanting to make a purchase when the product doesn't seem to fit.

"It happens a lot, but it shouldn't be taken for granted. Remember what we talked about yesterday: early adopters will purchase something that isn't a perfect fit and then work with you to make it better. We want to be careful and not overcommit to adding features or making changes to the product for customers who are not aligned with our strategy.

"Again, this is another aspect of being *fooled by early adopters,* where the wrong customers are setting the company's strategy. Spending valuable product development resources for a one-off customer that does not grow our share of our target market can seriously hinder success."

"That's exactly what I was thinking a few minutes ago when you said, 'what have we got to lose?'" Jonathan blurted out. "I just couldn't put words to it. Sometimes I feel like we're chasing down feature requests from current customers. and I wonder if it is taking us down the wrong path."

Parth nodded in agreement.

"It might be. That's why it's so critical to have a go-to-market strategy that defines what problems we're focused on solving now, and what problems are next. Without a clearly defined path, we won't know if a certain action takes us off the path we should be on or takes us in the direction we want to go."

Sensing a bit of closure on the topic, Parth moved to the final section of the diagram.

"The '*Validate*' step will differ depending on whether we make a sale or not. In both cases, we're asking the customer for their view of validation. Essentially asking them, 'What would it look like if this problem was solved?' and 'How would you measure success?'

"When we make a sale, validation comes from seeing our product solve their problem. Sales numbers alone don't create validation, we have to actually observe our product in the customer's hands."

Parth wrote '*Observe &*' above '*Validate*' before continuing. "From observing our product in use, we can confirm that we solve the customer's problem.

"On the other hand, if we do not solve the customer's problem in an efficient, cost-effective way, then we may need to adjust something in the process. Maybe a hypothesis is wrong, or our solution needs to change. Does that make sense?"

Everyone nodded in agreement.

Parth drew another arrow out from '*Validate*' and added '*Grow to MVM Leader*' with another arrow and '*Expand.*'

"Once we've validated the problem-solution alignment with enough customers and have grown to a market leadership position, then it's time to expand the minimum viable market to an adjacent market.

"Like I mentioned earlier, ultimate validation is the customer using our product to solve their problem and then being willing to talk about it. When that happens, it's much easier to grow our market share within our existing market and in adjacent markets."

Parth surveyed the group before asking, "Any questions about the customer discovery process overview?"

"How do you know when you're done and ready to scale the company?" Jonathan asked. "It seems like this could go on forever. What am I missing?"

"Well, there are a few ways to think about *done*," Parth began, "but when you are customer-focused, testing and validating assumptions is an ongoing process, especially when you introduce new features or go after new market segments."

Parth took a step back from the whiteboard and put the marker down. It was obvious he wanted to talk about the bigger picture. "Let's look at it from the perspective of scaling the company— before building a company, you want to first confirm that you have a product that solves a problem, and then that you can build a business around that product.

"The first part of customer development, customer discovery, is to find product fit. There are two primary questions for product fit. One, *is this a critical problem for a significant number of customers?* Two, *does our product solve the problem at a price that customers are willing to pay?*

"After customer discovery, customer validation is about finding business-model fit. There are many questions related to confirming business-model fit, covering topics from the value proposition to customer segments to cost structure and revenue streams."

"Another full day," Alex sighed as he leaned back in his chair. "I mean, I think we could do this for the rest of the year and not run out of talking points."

Everyone nodded at Alex's comment, and then Denise asked a question that was also on Jonathan's mind:

"So, I take it there's no 'one size fits all' solution to product/market fit, is there?"

Jonathan would have asked that question with a completely different tone of voice. Something more desperate than inquisitive. If anything, Denise looked like her own beliefs had finally been validated.

"That's right." Parth nodded his head. "There's a process that can be widely applied, but no 'one size fits all' way to look at it. As you can probably imagine, an e-commerce company is very different from an app, which is very different from what SyncAnalytix does. And industrial IoT is different from consumer IoT.

"A better way to look at it is to envision what your ideal business is, figure out the basic assumptions you have about the business, and then chart a path from where you are now to the ideal. If we had more time, we would work through the Lean Canvas framework or something similar, but we'll save that for next time.

"What we'll talk about this afternoon is how you can chart a path towards finding product fit."

Parth was ready to transition to a new topic but surveyed the team to see if they were ready to leave the discovery discussion, or if they still needed more time. After how much they'd covered already, he could tell that if he immediately led them somewhere new, a good amount of information could get lost. He set his marker down.

"We're at a good spot to take a break. Does anyone have more questions on what we just covered?"

All three of them relaxed. Jonathan thought about the cup of coffee he wanted to get in his hands as soon as he left the conference room. And then Denise chimed in:

"I know I have plenty of questions, but they're probably too detailed to spend time on them today," she said. "Do you have a list of resources we can look into later?"

"Definitely," Parth answered with a smile. "Depending on how deep you want to go, there's an infinite number of resources out there."

Jonathan knew Parth meant that to be encouraging, but in the spirit of honesty...

"See, that's what overwhelms me," he interjected. "Where would we even start?"

"I'll recommend a few places you can start. It'll probably turn out to be less overwhelming than you think. After talking through these concepts in the context of SyncAnalytix, things will make more sense now that you have something to hang the information on."

"Well," Alex said. He stood up. "I recommend we start by taking that break Parth mentioned."

"Good idea," Parth said. "Let's meet back here in fifteen minutes. When we get back, we'll review our basic assumptions and discuss a strategy for measuring and tracking progress towards verifying those assumptions."

17
LEARN

As expected, the short break gave all of them the energy they needed to dig back into product/market fit. They found their seats around the conference table like it was a new day, even getting carried away talking about their weekend plans before Parth restarted their discussion.

"Okay, let's go back through some of the assumptions we have about the problem, customer, and market."

Parth started pointing to the different sections of the board. "For the problem, we landed on system failure, system downtime, and performance. System failure is the biggest problem and ultimate solution to focus on," he continued, "but solving that problem with analytics requires technical leadership in the market, which is hard for an early-stage startup."

Parth circled '*system failure*' and turned to look at Jonathan.

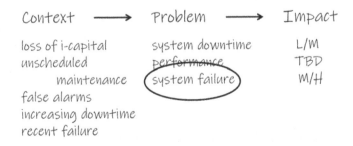

"The question here is, can we map out a strategy that starts with addressing false alarms, builds through solving system downtime, and eventually creates the credibility needed to be a strong contender for the system failure solution?" Parth asked.

Jonathan figured that had to be a rhetorical question. "Of course we can. I'm still trying to understand why we should change our current focus when we're so close to solving all three of those for customers."

"I can think of some reasons why we should follow Parth's advice here," Alex offered. "We're a little early to the market to offer a full analytics solution. It's just too risky to focus on sales there without being a clear market leader."

"But it's a perfect opportunity for us to *become* the market leader," Jonathan cut in.

Alex winced slightly.

"Honestly, it *sounds* like a great opportunity, but I think it's just too much. We're understaffed and overcommitted right now. Trying to shoot for market leadership with our current resources would be a stretch. We're probably years from having that level of technical credibility with potential customers."

Those were words he'd never heard from Alex, but Jonathan could tell he'd been thinking about these issues for longer than just the past few days. It just took Parth coming in and upending their strategy to get his thoughts out.

"But a lot of the deals we've lost recently have been to competitors like OscarIoT, not major technology companies." Jonathan added.

"Well, that's true," Alex replied. "But those deals will end in implementation failure and then they'll be forced to hire a major anyway, since no one in their right mind would engage a second startup after the first one failed."

Denise looked over at Parth. "Are we getting off track?" she asked.

"It's starting to sound like it, isn't it," Jonathan admitted.

Parth responded, "Actually, I would say the opposite. This is exactly the kind of conversation you should be having as an executive team at this stage of the company. Do you have anything you want to add?" he asked Denise.

Denise thought for a moment. She didn't usually witness the discussions Jonathan and Alex had in the Sales meetings, and her ideas during this discussion seemed to conflict with the direction Jonathan was heading.

Still, she trusted that it would be better to speak up now.

She cleared her throat. "From my perspective, if we could make some changes to our product that would put us in the role of primary vendor, then we would be better positioned to offer our solution to system failure when it is ready. If we prove we can solve the first two problems better than anyone in the market, then I think it would be reasonable to start offering a full analytics solution."

"You think so?" Jonathan asked. He was surprised by how much she seemed to have thought this through, which made him realize he needed to give his team more credit for thinking strategically.

Denise nodded. "If you're a plant manager and your SyncAnalytix software consistently reduces system downtime, who are you going to engage with when addressing system failure becomes available?"

"Us," Jonathan said.

Alex agreed with her as well. "I definitely think that's the best way to go," he said. "And we would have six to nine months of analytics data on which to build robust models."

After Alex and Jonathan agreed with Denise, Parth circled '*system downtime*' and drew an arrow to '*system failure.*'

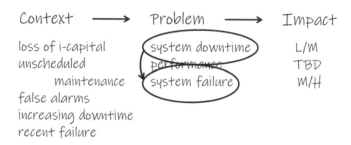

"*And* we would know their systems inside and out," Denise continued. "Let's let OscarIoT fight it out with the rest of the market as a supporting vendor while we focus on solving real problems for the customer."

The dig at OscarIoT earned a satisfied affirmation out of Alex.

"Now I'm starting to love this idea."

"Me too," Jonathan said.

"Alright, sounds like we agree on the problem space and a strategy to go after a minimum viable market," Parth continued. "This diagram is the 'build-measure-learn' feedback loop you may have heard of. The key point here is to work with customers during each step."

Parth quickly wrote '*Build*,' '*Measure*,' and '*Learn*' on the board and connected each word with an arrow.

"Once we've tested as much as we can through customer interviews and market analysis, build-measure-learn is how we validate that the product solves the customer's problem," Parth said. Then he drew the three arrows. "The discussion we just had needs to be validated with customers before any action is taken to redesign the product or launch a full go-to-market strategy."

"If the three of us agree, though, it seems like a waste of time to ask customers to confirm it for us," Jonathan protested. "I mean, at least with more obvious ideas. We know this technology better than anyone."

"Well, I agree," Parth responded, "to an extent, it might seem like a waste of time..." He paused for emphasis.

"...if we are *right*. But if we're wrong, or even just slightly wrong, talking with customers will help you avoid going after a flawed strategy which could be an even bigger waste of time."

"That makes sense to me," Denise said. "Thinking we had all the right answers probably got us where we are now—stuck."

Jonathan looked around the room. Parth hadn't exactly reassured him about the time issue. He was an engineer, after all, not a philosopher. And he had a company to run. He wanted more assurance that talking to customers would result in a different outcome. Finally, he sighed.

"I think you have a point, Denise. It's true that everything felt *right* until we started feeling stuck."

"There can be a fine line between the perfect strategy and one that misses the mark completely," Parth said. "I think the build-measure-learn concept is straightforward, but what gets challenging is how to measure and track progress.

"Too many startups go from an idea to a product and then measure success with sales."

Parth drew a simple diagram on the board to emphasize his point.

Idea ⟶ Product ⟶ Sales

"Measuring the success of your product with a sales number doesn't provide a lot of actionable feedback—other than 'we need to sell more.'"

Jonathan shifted uneasily in his chair, wondering what the company should focus on if not the sales number.

"The goal today is to define a plan for finding product/market fit so we can have the confidence that we *are* spending the right money on the right things at the right time - how we confirm we are solving the customer's problem in a cost-efficient way, so they avoid the impact or consequences of not solving their problem.

"What we've discussed the past two days are hypotheses—which can only take you so far without an idea of how to test and validate them. These feed into the '*Build*' part of the loop," Parth added as he wrote "*Hypotheses*" above '*Build*'.

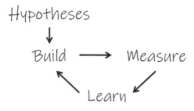

"Ah ha," Denise said. "I've wondered why lean startup always uses the term 'hypotheses.' It always seemed like an odd choice."

"I know it sounds scientific," Parth replied, "but it really works to describe what we've been talking about. A lot of the things we might have assumed are facts are not actually facts until we have tested and validated them, which is the '*Learn*' section of the diagram leading to '*Insights*.'"

Parth wrote '*Insights*' below '*Learn*.'

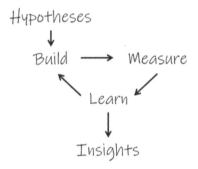

"Whoa, hold on," Jonathan said. "The hypothesis thing—that's the stuff that keeps me up at night. What I just *assumed* was true, but for whatever reason, doesn't actually seem to be working."

"I think we've all been losing sleep," Alex added. "If there's a way to fix that, I'm all in."

Parth let everyone think over the idea of *validating hypotheses* in relation to their shared anxiety for a few more seconds before he continued.

"In theory," he said, "the minimum viable product is supposed to help founders validate their hypotheses, a tool for testing assumptions about the problem. Some companies took this concept in a different direction, and it ended up as just a new name for the beta release of traditional product development. Eventually the

MVP concept became so confused and watered down that when founders say, 'we have an MVP,' it's actually an excuse for releasing an incomplete product with no clear goal, other than hoping to exceed $100,000 a month in revenue as soon as possible."

"We don't have an incomplete product," Jonathan countered. He realized too late how defensive his statement sounded. He tried again. "But I will admit I'm starting to see where we might have skipped over the work of verifying that we were on the right track." Jonathan thought back to Vaughn's question about 'the right time to scale.' He'd been convinced that 'validation' would come as a result of meeting their sales quotas.

He made a note to buy Vaughn lunch so he could give a better answer to his 'right time to scale' question. *After* they had a better form of market validation, of course.

"I haven't been doing the kind of work that would validate our expectations about the product either," Denise added. "I understand why the focus is on sales, though. Even though I should be rooting for more resources in Marketing, I'm not sure how we can validate something other than through sales."

"I'm wondering that too," Alex added. "Not that I'm trying to shirk any responsibility for not meeting quota."

Jonathan was still stuck thinking about the 'right time to scale.' He had a feeling in the back of his mind that he was just *this* close to figuring out the answer.

Alex continued, "It sounds like finding product/market fit requires that we do more than set a quota for the Sales Team."

"That's what I've learned from working with other startups on this exact issue," Parth confirmed. "Sometimes quantitative targets will drive qualitative inquiry which can lead to validated learning. Not always, though, and I prefer to plan the steps that ensure we're on the right path. Let's start with the three major hypotheses we came up with."

Parth gestured to the different sections of the board he'd written on, to all their assumptions on the customer, the problem, and the cost of the problem—which Jonathan understood now as their *hypotheses*.

"Now someone stop me if I get anything wrong in the recap of the last couple of days," he said. "The *customer* hypothesis is 'the ideal customer is a plant manager at a company that has seen a recent failure or increase in system downtime.'

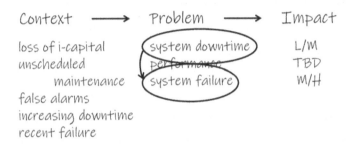

Context ⟶ Problem ⟶ Impact

Context	Problem	Impact
loss of i-capital	system downtime	L/M
unscheduled	performance	TBD
maintenance	system failure	M/H
false alarms		
increasing downtime		
recent failure		

"The *problem* hypothesis is 'false alarms and unscheduled maintenance lead to system downtime and, in extreme cases, system failure.'

"The *value* hypothesis is 'customers can reduce system downtime with an IoT analytics system that has robust sensor data models and better anomaly detection.'"

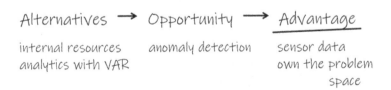

Alternatives ⟶ Opportunity ⟶ Advantage

Alternatives	Opportunity	Advantage
internal resources	anomaly detection	sensor data
analytics with VAR		own the problem
		space

The three of them were nodding through his summary. Jonathan felt a surge of energy from hearing all their assumptions spoken so clearly, after what now felt like months of flying blind. But even though they hadn't defined them *out loud*, wasn't that what they were already working on anyway?

"The customer hypothesis, the problem hypothesis, and the value hypothesis," Alex repeated. "That almost makes it sound easy."

Parth turned around after he finished pointing to the output of their brainstorming. "Sometimes these statements feel too simplistic to be worth spending time on, especially with the whole executive team. Would you agree, Jonathan?"

"Now that you mention it," Jonathan started, "they do seem a little underwhelming. We have deep technical expertise, but these statements don't seem to reflect any of that. I have a feeling you have something more to say about that."

"We've spent too much time in this room, you're all starting to catch on to my leading questions." Parth smiled.

"There's usually an effort to make the statements more technical or more product focused, but the point I want to make is that customers care more about solving their immediate problems than about the possibilities of your product.

"These three statements are not just a one-and-done exercise, but instead form the basis of an ongoing process of building competitive intelligence about the problem, the customer, and our value proposition. Now that we all agree on the basics, we can develop these further over the coming weeks as you meet with customers and learn more about what they need."

"I get it," Denise offered. "Most of our competitors could come up with the same information. The next step is for us to take this information to a deeper level in order to understand our customers like no one else."

"Correct," Parth said. "It's what we decide to do next that makes all the difference. Do we move forward and build out our intelligence around the problem, customer, and value proposition? Or do we go back to a product focus where we continually add features hoping to stumble upon the right combination to close more sales?"

Jonathan recognized the second strategy option Parth mentioned, maybe a little too well.

"I think we're all tired of the way we were doing things before," he said as he looked at Denise and Alex. "As much as I love adding complexity to our product, I'm open to trying this approach. What do you guys think?"

"I'm here because you're a technical genius," Denise began, "but we don't seem to be getting the market traction we deserve. I think we can change that with this approach. So, I'm all in."

"Ditto for me," Alex said. "On all points."

Jonathan was at a loss for words, and not because he felt out of his depth as a leader. This time, it was the opposite. Maybe even for the first time since he started this company.

He nodded to Parth to continue.

"Great," Parth responded enthusiastically. "Most of that work will happen outside this building, especially while meeting with customers, but let's spend the remaining time we have today discussing a strategy towards validating these different hypotheses."

"Can we start with the customer hypothesis?" Denise asked. "Or would it be better to define an MVP and work backwards from the value hypothesis?"

"At this point we've done more than our fair share of starting with the product," Jonathan cut in, which actually made Denise smile. "I think it's time to try it from the customer side of things."

"I vote for customer as well," Alex added. "If we can nail down the customer, our Sales Team will have a much better focus going forward."

"You have the floor, Denise. What do you think we would need to do to validate the customer hypothesis?" Parth asked.

Denise skimmed back through her notes for a minute before deciding on her answer.

"It seems to me that a lot of this would fall on Alex's department, but don't we essentially just need to talk to customers, see if they experience the problem as we define it, and determine if they would find our solution worth the cost? Make sure we can confirm the whole 'ready,' 'willing,' 'able,' and 'made successful' list?"

"Yes," Parth began, "but be careful how you approach the cost question. In the discovery phase, we're not looking for pricing feedback exactly, but something I call 'value intelligence.' We want to understand what *value* customers will realize from solving the problem, how much they may have spent trying to solve it, and how much they could save by solving the problem. If a customer is not willing to spend money to solve their problem, then we haven't identified a real problem."

"Sounds like we should be running focus groups," Jonathan countered.

"In the grand scheme of things, that *is* what we need to do," Parth explained, looking over at Jonathan. "Ideally, we'll be taking the tools of a skilled focus group facilitator into the discovery meetings with customers. By asking questions about the problem, we can confirm customer alignment with our hypotheses."

Alex looked deep in thought. "This sounds like solution-selling rather than target-account-selling."

"What's the difference?" Jonathan asked.

"Solution-selling is based on learning and problem-solving. There are a few variations, but all of them focus on partnering with the customer to solve their problem. Target-account-selling is about identifying the customer, building a relationship with them, and looking for opportunities to sell our product." Alex started to shake his head. "We've been following the target account model—more selling, less learning."

"That sounds right," Parth added. "Identifying early adopters without using a problem-solving focus is difficult because they can be in any role in the organization. The key to recognizing them is that they understand their problem, are actively looking for a solution, and have the relational capital within the organization to try new things.

"We'll need to use tactics from both sales strategies, but strict target account selling works best with known products in known markets with known buyers."

Jonathan sighed. He knew the implication there. "That's not us, is it?" he asked.

Denise shook her head no.

Alex continued. "Considering that most people don't understand what we're selling and that the buyer changes from company to company, I would guess we're not working with known buyers in known markets."

"Right," Denise continued, "and it's hard to apply standard marketing methods to a market that's still developing."

Parth agreed as well. "Most of what business programs teach has to do with marketing to the majority—the center of the bell curve—very little is taught about how to transition from early adopters to the mainstream market."

Bringing the focus back to validating the customer hypothesis, Parth asked, "What specific actions can we take to learn more about the customer?"

"We need to ask questions about how the customer is experiencing the problem and what they believe the root causes are," Alex offered.

"And how they try to solve that problem," Jonathan added.

"Right." Alex nodded.

"And what they experience by not solving the problem," Denise added. And then she paused for a moment.

"I'm still not sure if changing how we talk to customers will confirm our assumptions about the customer."

"Well, we've identified some actions, but we also need to come up with some metrics that we can track as a team," Parth responded. "Just like metrics around shifting the marketing message on a website—click throughs, opens, time on site, that sort of thing. The Sales Team also needs to develop a standard set of questions and track responses for confirmation or contradiction.

"It's starting to sound like we should be talking about these things way more often," Jonathan said. "Or is that just me?"

"I think that'll make a huge difference around here," Denise said.

Parth nodded. "I agree. I always recommend that these conversations continue after we finish this meeting."

"Speaking of which, we still have some more work to do. How do we address the problem hypothesis?" Jonathan asked.

"As the technical and product lead, you need to understand the customer experience—the what, why, and when that would cause a customer to look for a solution," Parth responded.

"Before changing the product to move into a primary vendor position, we should get customer feedback from the perspective of solving the full problem and then consider creating a mock-up of the solution."

"As part of the customer meetings?" Alex asked.

"Probably not the first interaction," Parth responded, "but when we qualify a customer and there's alignment on the problem hypotheses, we should plan for the discovery team to spend time with them to dig deeper into the problem and how we could solve it as the primary vendor."

"So, similar to the customer side of things, we need a set of questions in order to see how they respond?"

"Yes," Parth replied, "but this is also where the MVP concept comes into play. We need to—with the help of early adopters—define a minimum viable product that will allow our customers to start solving their problem. It doesn't need to be a full solution, with a beautiful UX running on multiple platforms, but it does need to create value for the customer."

"Like fixing downtime on specific equipment or a specific production process?" Jonathan asked.

"That might be an option," Parth said. "The minimum viable market concept we discussed will also help define an MVP. By focusing on a specific problem, we can really start to nail the solution."

Parth shifted his focus back to customer interviews.

"As part of digging into the problem, it's important to ask customers how they intend to measure success. Some of that information will come from the initial discussions, some from understanding what consequences they experience and how those consequences impact productivity measures. Then, if possible, those measurement methods need to be designed into the product."

"What do you mean by 'measurement methods' being designed into the product?" Jonathan asked.

"I'm glad you asked." Parth smiled. Jonathan could sense that he was walking down a well-worn path, after all the protests he'd made. "This gets overlooked because we assume that buying and using the product should be enough of a 'result.' Instead of assuming we solve the problem, how could we capture and present 'results' that show the problem is being solved? To us and to customers."

"Showing metrics such as machine uptime or overall equipment efficiency," Jonathan offered. "Is that what you mean?"

"It could be," Parth continued, "and that sounds like a good place to start. Depending on the complexity of the system, success metrics can be difficult to capture, but the product itself should provide as much confirmation of value as possible to the customer."

"That totally makes sense," Alex added. "Instead of hoping they can see the value on their own, show them the benefits they receive every day. The more we can get success data from our own system, the more we know about how we deliver on our value proposition. I love it!"

Parth nodded at Alex's answer. "So, as we're interviewing customers, we're asking what metrics they'll use to evaluate success, and then providing those directly from the product whenever possible."

"We've talked about some of this already, but is everyone ready to move on to the value hypothesis?" Parth asked the group, anticipating there would be no objections.

Everyone nodded.

Normally if a meeting ran this long, across multiple days, the energy would have started to decline by this point, and Jonathan would be thinking about how much work he had waiting for him at his computer. Needless to say, today was a very different day at SyncAnalytix.

"So, in determining the value of our product, an easy metric to measure is revenue in the form of monthly or annual license fees. But, as we discussed earlier, revenue is a lag measure and doesn't give us direct feedback on our value proposition. What other metrics could we use that provide direct feedback?

"For example, is there a way to get customers to talk about success with the product? Word-of-mouth referrals are critical to build technical credibility. Do plant managers talk with other plant managers?"

"Some do," Jonathan began, "but that can be industry-specific. Some plants consider production methods proprietary."

"That makes sense. Not all success information can be communicated outside the company but be on the lookout for ones that can.

"We want to think about how to move customers from being adopters to advocates and then brand ambassadors for SyncAnalytix."

"The retention side of the bow tie funnel," Denise offered.

Parth nodded in agreement.

"What is an advocate and a brand ambassador?" Jonathan asked Denise.

"It's when our customers are finding new customers for us."

"Exactly," Parth added. "When we're working with early adopters, we need more than the initial sale. We need the sale, the renewal, and help finding more customers.

"We can discuss more over lunch, but early adopters who become brand ambassadors are an indication that we're on our way to product/market fit."

Jonathan turned in his chair to check the time.

"Speaking of lunchtime, it should almost be here. Let's take a quick break and I'll go check on where it is," Jonathan said as he stood up from the table.

"I never thought about brand ambassadors as signals of product/market fit," Denise said enthusiastically as Jonathan left the room to find their lunch order.

"Yes," Parth added with a smile. "We can develop a few of these ideas further over lunch and then talk about how to build out a go-to-market strategy and track progress."

"Go-to-market progress, now that's my favorite thing to track," Alex said.

18

LEAPS

After a short break, Jonathan returned with everyone's lunch order. Instead of taking a break over lunch, they ended up discussing how to meet with customers, test hypotheses, and turn early adopters into brand ambassadors. Here and there, Alex offered his thoughts on how previous customer meetings might have affirmed or contradicted some of their hypotheses. Parth shared a few anecdotes where startups had solved problems in unique and powerful ways which caused their customers to become committed to the startups' success, thus leading to strong referrals. Jonathan started to envision SyncAnalytix reaching that point with customers.

Once everyone finished their lunch and the conversation began to wane, Parth returned to the meeting agenda.

"So," he said, getting up from the table, "as you're going through the build-measure-learn loop with multiple customers, it's important to track metrics that can show progress.

"This part gets really nuanced and specific to the three hypotheses we already have and the strategic direction we want to take the company. Behind the problem, customer, and value hypotheses are some assumptions about each that need to be articulated, tested and validated. These assumptions are called leap-of-faith assumptions."

"Leap-of-faith in what way?" Jonathan asked.

"Sometimes in a big way," Parth responded. "In those cases, you can think of it as a bet-the-company kind of assumption. In general, leap-of-faith assumptions drive the actions you take whether you say them out loud or not. So, it's important that we articulate these assumptions, figure out a fast and easy way to test them, and then measure the results to see if we're right or wrong."

"Is it like identifying where the risks are?" Denise asked.

"It's similar," Parth began, "but a little different. A risk is something that involves failure or loss. So, by identifying risks, we articulate what we want to avoid. A leap-of-faith assumption is usually something good that we think will happen. For example, we believe that the plant manager will spend $60,000 on our software to solve a problem that is costing them $150,000 per incident."

"Sounds like a positive affirmation before going into a sales meeting," Alex offered.

Parth nodded with a smile. "I guess it could be. I never thought of it that way, but you could say it's the positive stuff we tell ourselves will happen in relation to the problem, product, customer, and value proposition."

"So, for the product," Jonathan began, "a leap-of-faith assumption could be that our sensor data provides a competitive advantage in machine learning."

"Tell us more about that." Parth encouraged Jonathan. "In what way do you think that's a leap-of-faith?"

Jonathan thought for a few seconds before offering more detail.

"Well, we did a pilot for a customer, and we were able to train their algorithms faster because we had existing sensor data. They were able to get up and running four days faster, but I don't know if the speed was worth it to the customer."

"Sounds like you can prove that sensor data provides a benefit. Maybe the leap-of-faith in this case is whether or not the customer cares. The leap-of-faith assumption might be 'the plant manager derives value from decreasing initial implementation time by four days.' How does that sound?"

"Sounds right," Jonathan said as he nodded his head. "I can prove that we got the customer up and running faster, I guess the leap I made was that the time savings provides value."

Jonathan could think of a few areas where he just assumed a technically superior product would provide value.

"Got some more in there?" Parth asked.

"Probably more than I care to admit," Jonathan answered. "I mean, what we listed as alternative weaknesses the other day, or competitive advantages—like sensor data—those could be leap-of-faith assumptions, right?"

"Right! That's where startups get ahead of themselves. We each walk into a meeting or a customer engagement with a set of assumptions. Any assumption the customer remotely endorses gets converted into fact in our mind."

"We hear what we want to hear in an effort to confirm our assumptions? Is that what you are saying?" Alex asked.

"I can't reference any studies off the top of my head," Parth started, glancing at Jonathan. "But essentially, we hear what we want to hear. And worse, if we hear the opposite, we disregard it. I've actually heard founders say, 'we just need to talk to more customers' even though every customer they talk to says the opposite of what they want to hear."

Parth smiled and shook his head. "So, we end up having our unarticulated assumptions reinforced subconsciously. Even if it's a sample size of one, it's now true and starts driving the wrong actions. String enough wrong actions together, we end up executing a bad strategy that takes the company—"

"—down a death spiral." Jonathan interrupted, finishing Parth's sentence.

"Yes! Exactly," Parth exclaimed as he pointed his marker in Jonathan's direction. "I was thinking 'down the wrong path', but 'death spiral' is way more descriptive. Let's avoid the death spiral, everyone."

Denise and Alex waited to hear what Jonathan would say next. Ethan's presentation was not exactly a bright day in the company's history, and the whole 'death spiral' idea seemed to be haunting Jonathan for days afterwards.

From the first meeting a few days ago, Parth had been passionate about helping SyncAnalytix avoid the mistakes he had seen other founders make. Jonathan had a sense that unarticulated assumptions and unstated hypotheses were clearly a hot button for him.

"Maybe if we had met six months ago, we could have avoided the death spiral," Jonathan added.

"You know, I hear that a lot, but I don't know if that's true." Parth responded. "Sometimes founders have to hit the wall before they're willing to make the changes required to follow lean startup methodology. And anyway, *now* is a great time to get things back on track."

"I just want to find our way out of the death spiral before it's too late."

Jonathan couldn't help but go back to dwelling on the term 'death spiral'. Even after how motivating the past few hours had been.

"We will, and I definitely don't think it's too late," Parth reassured Jonathan.

Jonathan felt some comfort in Parth's reassurance. He still didn't see a path forward, but all the different points Parth had been making the past few days were like little puzzle pieces that were just starting to come together in his head. It made him feel better to know that everything was already *there*, they just had to assemble the pieces into a full picture.

He let out the breath he'd been holding, and with it, the term 'death spiral'.

"So, where do we go from here?"

"Well, I think you understand the leap-of-faith assumptions enough that each of you could write a few down. Is that right?" Parth asked, looking over to Alex and Denise.

Both nodded in agreement.

"I can definitely think of multiple positive affirmations I use that could be considered leaps-of-faith." Alex added.

Parth directed his next statement to Jonathan.

"I don't know if you're doing detailed financial forecasting, but if you are, we can look at some key variables in the model and see which ones have the biggest impact or most sensitivity."

"We're not doing that yet, but we are supposed to build out a more detailed forecast for next year. What kind of things should we look for?" Jonathan asked.

"Some typical things I see for software businesses are assumptions around cost-to-acquire customers, conversion rates, retention...actually, when you think about it, even the average selling price can be a leap-of-faith assumption until you have some history that confirms what the market is willing to pay.

"In general, the more sensitive the forecast model is to a single variable, the sooner you want to validate that variable."

"Ok," Jonathan continued, "so we come up with our list of leaps, then what?"

"Then we map them on a four-quadrant matrix."

Parth turned and drew two lines which formed a typical X and Y axis on the board. On the vertical axis, he wrote '*Impact*' and on the horizontal axis, he wrote '*Time*'.

"This a cross between an Eisenhower Matrix and a BCG Growth-Share Matrix," Parth said as he wrote '*Low*' and '*Long*' in the lower left-hand corner, '*High*' on the top left, and '*Short*' on the bottom right. He finished his diagram by drawing a perfect circle in the upper right-hand quadrant of the chart.

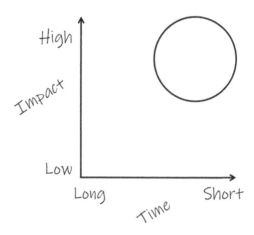

"Once we agree on some of the biggest or most important leaps," Parth said as he turned to Jonathan. "I actually like that--*leaps*-- I think I'm going to start using that."

"Then," he continued, "we take the ten to twenty most important leaps and map them across these two dimensions.

As an example, Parth wrote '*L1*' through '*L6*' randomly around the chart as he continued talking. "Leap-of-faith assumptions that have a high impact and a short time to impact are what we want to focus on."

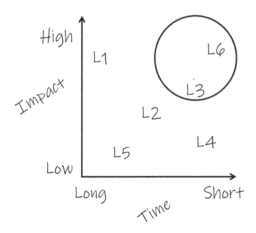

Parth finished his sentence by pointing to the circle.

"Areas outside of this circle, leaps with a low impact or a long time to impact, should receive less focus. We want to reduce the maximum amount of risk with the minimum amount of investment.

"So, in this example, we would focus on leap-of-faith assumptions three and six."

"And how does that work?" Denise asked. "I mean, what does it mean to focus on a leap-of-faith assumption in the upper right-hand corner?"

"With each leap," Parth said with a smile as if Jonathan had defined a new term, "we define a test and a measure. Some test measure combinations will be as simple as asking customers and tabulating responses. Some tests will require the customer to buy and utilize an MVP.

"Using what I previously called a leap-of-faith scoring chart, which will now be the '*leap scoring chart*,'" Parth said as he drew some more lines on the board.

	CI-1	MA-1	MVP-1	MVP-2	PF-1
L1		X		X	
L2	X				
L3			X		
L4				X	X
L5				X	
L6			X		

"This is similar to a feature comparison matrix, except across the top you list different test methods. For example, Customer Interview, Market Analysis, MVPs, Product Feature. Then, on the left-hand side you list the leaps; for example, '*L1*' through '*L6*'. If a particular MVP can test three leaps, then you check those rows. If adding a feature to the existing product can test a different set of leaps, then you check those rows." Parth finished his chart by placing an 'X' in a few random locations.

"These two charts help prioritize what we should be working on and what assumptions we're trying to address. I like to group these different leap-of-faith assumptions by considering the strategy needed to get a majority share of the target market within 12 to 18 months. They can also help prioritize decisions around the product roadmap."

"So," Denise began, "in your example, we would use these two charts to build a go-to-market strategy starting with MVP-1?"

"Yes," Parth responded. "There may be two or three minimum viable markets that seem equally attractive. We use the newly-named *leap* prioritization chart and *leap* scoring chart to decide which one has the greatest probability of success."

Parth looked at Jonathan as if he expected him to respond to a specific point he had just made.

"I know what you're about to say," Jonathan conceded. "We only focus on one market at a time, no matter how attractive going after all three markets at once may seem."

Jonathan sat back and felt his mind racing. It was as if the past two and a half days were a marathon discussion of explaining the past and they just ran a half mile sprint through the future.

"My head is spinning," Denise spoke up first. "I think I see a path forward, though. I mean, I also see a lot of work, but work with a purpose. Does that make sense?"

Jonathan was still busy processing multiple thoughts from different directions and was happy to let the rest of his team take the reins.

"It makes sense to me," Alex began, "I feel like we've been spinning our wheels the past six months and making very little progress."

Alex stood up to stretch his legs. "But to play devil's advocate for a moment, how do we know this is going to be any different? How do we know that after trying this plan for the next three months we aren't just spinning a different set of wheels?"

Parth thought for a moment before answering Alex.

"The big difference, as I see it, is that before now, SyncAnalytix was iterating on finding sales. If a certain sales method didn't work or a customer segment didn't work, then you tried a new one. A product looking for a market. What I've given you a glimpse of is how to iterate on delivering value. When we find how to deliver value to customers by solving their problem, sales will follow.

"I don't think of myself as a lean manufacturing expert, but, as I mentioned before, my understanding is that lean manufacturing is about taking waste out of the manufacturing process. A big waste in manufacturing is poor quality. When you increase the quality you eliminate waste — and create more value for the customer. Same idea."

Something clicked for Jonathan that seemed to tie everything together. He rejoined the conversation.

"The big thing I think we've been wasting is our collective efforts—our ability to co-create. I heard a talk recently, and the point I took away was that I need to get stuff out of my head and share it with others."

"With you," Jonathan said looking at Denise.

"And with you," he said to Alex. "All of us, working as a team.

"These leap-of-faith assumptions influence the actions we take. If we don't know each other's assumptions, we can't interpret each other's actions. So, we end up working in silos.

"And if we don't have alignment as a team, how can we create alignment with customers? Forget about 'fit', we won't get past where we are now without actually finding alignment and creating new possibilities together."

Jonathan sighed.

"And to Alex's question about whether this is just another management theory that will have us spinning our wheels again in six months, my guess is no. And not just because I hope that won't be the case. Everything Parth has said has lined up with our past experience, and the whole part about being 'fooled by early adopters' is way too accurate.

"These leap charts—which I'm going to copyright by the way," Jonathan said with a smile to Parth. "These exercises are going to help us get aligned and participating in the same reality."

Jonathan paused. He felt a sort of energy running through him, and knew he needed to finish his point.

"That's what's been holding us back all this time. I think if we can find that—alignment, shared reality, whatever you want to call it—this company could be something great."

"I agree," Denise said, and Jonathan realized that what he felt, what he'd been feeling whenever the whole team had found common ground today, was pride, after months of insecurity and doubt. Looking at Alex and Denise, he could tell he wasn't the only one.

"I always thought this was an awesome team," Alex added. "We've got this!"

"You guys have done an amazing job going through all these details.," Parth said with a big smile, "On that note, I think we can wrap up for today. I know we had to move quickly, but I think you have the basics down and know where to go from here in your future meetings."

"I agree," Jonathan said as he leaned back in his chair. "I wish we did this six months ago, but you were probably right that I might not have been open to it."

"Wow! I think Jonathan's motivational speech had some great words to end on," Denise said, "Parth, you've really revolutionized this place in just three days."

"I'll say," Alex chimed in, "this is all my team is going to be hearing about for weeks."

Parth smiled and nodded. "It's all about asking the right questions. The three of you had the information when we first started, you just needed to put it out there as a team and think about it differently."

"That gives me hope for when we have to have more of these meetings without you here to moderate," Jonathan said.

"Ha!" Parth laughed. "You'll see. Once you make it a regular part of the process, you won't be able to imagine this company without all this talk about hypotheses, expectations, and *leaps*."

For the first time in a long time, Jonathan didn't feel nervous, or anxious, about the future of the company. He felt excited to see what the team was capable of when they were fully aligned on creating new possibilities together.

19
DEBRIEF

A little before 2pm, Jonathan dialed Helen's number to start his weekly coaching call. After exchanging some chitchat with Marsha, Jonathan was transferred to Helen's office phone.

"So, bring me up to speed on what's been happening over the last week. I'm curious to hear how the meeting with Parth went," Helen said to start them off.

After three days with Parth walking through lean startup concepts, the weekend felt like a blur. So many thoughts were racing through Jonathan's mind that it was difficult for him to be present with his family, let alone relax and stop thinking about work. He distracted himself for hours with his Charger rebuild—a project that had stalled for months during the long work hours and stress of SyncAnalytix missing forecast again and again. Still, it was a different kind of stress than he usually dealt with over the weekend. This time he *knew* there was a way out, they just had to create it.

"There's so much we went over; I don't even know where to start." Jonathan sighed.

"How about starting with the most exciting thing you learned."

He was caught off guard by Helen's question. He could think of a few surprises and some discouraging realizations, but the word 'exciting' didn't bring anything to mind, at least not right away. Jonathan thought about the realization that the market they were going after was much smaller than they had been telling investors, and that was before further refinement to get to a minimum viable market.

He thought about Parth's comment that they were delivering a product that was more appropriately considered a solution to an implementation problem and not what the customer viewed as the solution to their primary problem.

'Exciting' probably didn't describe the realization that a lot of their actions were wasting time and sending them down the wrong path. That finding product/market fit would take them through multiple stages from 'match' to 'alignment'. Or, the sobering realization, that they may never reach 'fit'.

"I think the most exciting thing I learned," Jonathan began, hoping that his wandering mind would be able to finish his sentence sooner rather than later, "is that I don't need to fire my Sales VP."

Before Jonathan had time to second-guess his response, Helen moved the conversation forward.

"Well, considering that was where we started weeks ago, thinking you needed to fire Alex, I would say that *is* pretty exciting. What led you to that realization?"

Jonathan relaxed. He felt more comfortable talking about what was wrong or what problems needed to be fixed. Thinking and talking about the positives almost felt uncomfortable.

"I guess I thought that designing the product was the hardest thing about starting a company. Once I realized how complicated go-to-market strategy is, I understood that it wasn't Alex who was the obstacle, it was our lack of strategy that was leading us to failure."

Jonathan reflected on some of the conversations he had with Vaughn and other investors when SyncAnalytix was raising their Series A.

"I told investors that the hard part was over," Jonathan continued. "That we had a product in the market and sales were increasing. That all I needed was to hire Sales and Marketing, and our business would explode."

Jonathan shook his head, sensing his discouragement building.

"I even told some investors: 'look at this forecast model, it's pretty clear that we have a billion-dollar opportunity'. I never would have guessed that the biggest challenge comes after the product is built. I'm starting to wonder if designing and building a product is actually the *easiest* part."

"Let's not dwell on the past." Helen offered. "What are you doing with your team to put the right strategy in place?"

Jonathan's mood lifted as he thought of the leadership team meeting they had had earlier in the day. There was a new level of motivation between the three of them as they started to put their lessons from Parth into action.

"Wait," Jonathan interjected. "I want to go back to the first question. The most exciting thing is how capable our team actually is once our focus is aligned."

"Did this alignment come from Parth last week?"

"Yes. Well, maybe. I mean, Parth gave us the tools and worked through some simple examples. At the end of three days, I had some thoughts about how to move forward, but it wasn't until this morning, when we had our first discovery team meeting, that everything started to really come together.

"I was too focused on the sales quota and had everyone trying to achieve that—no matter what. Turns out, Denise was wasting a lot of time building sales collateral, Alex was wasting time meeting with the wrong customers, and the development team was wasting time adding features in hopes of closing a sale.

"All of this wasted time came from not having a clear strategy of what problem we were solving, who our customer was, or how we were going to confirm that we delivered value."

"So," Helen began, "how were things different this morning?"

"This morning we started sharing the different leap-of-faith assumptions that we had about what we were trying to do. It was enlightening to know what Alex and Denise were thinking instead of just guessing. This whole time I'd been guessing about what was important to them and never even realized it. In a few cases I found out I was wrong and had assumed something else was going through their minds."

"How did the rest of your team respond to the sharing exercise this morning?"

Jonathan smiled. "They certainly enjoyed it more than me. I mean, it is awkward for me to share what I am thinking. They don't get to hear that a lot, so I could tell they were excited, but I mostly just felt uncomfortable."

"Why is that?"

"Because I might be wrong," Jonathan responded. "I think we've talked about this before. How I don't like sharing my thoughts unless I know I'm right."

"I believe we discussed it in a different context," Helen continued, "what's wrong with sharing your assumptions with the team, even if they might be wrong?"

"I've just always thought, as the CEO, my job was to be right."

There was a pause and Jonathan wondered whether Helen was taking notes or stuck on what to say next. *Aren't leaders always right?* Jonathan thought again to himself.

"Can I provide an observation," Helen asked.

"Sure," Jonathan responded. He was curious what was coming next, if she felt she needed to ask permission.

"When we first started meeting, you kept a lot of things close to your chest. You were clearly reluctant to share unless you knew the answer. A lot of what we talked about the first few sessions were the problems you needed to solve.

"Everything was a problem to solve, even your team. In fact, our first meeting was about whether or not Alex should be fired—a problem to solve."

Helen paused. Since there was no question, Jonathan figured she had more to say. He was right.

"We also talked about how one of your challenges was to set the right strategy—another problem to solve, but you agreed to talk with your team about it and get their thoughts.

"So, since you started doing that, and agreeing to the meeting with Ethan, and later Parth, you made yourself vulnerable. You opened up. Does that sound accurate?"

Jonathan thought back through the last few weeks.

"Yeah, you're right. I heard a lot of stuff I didn't want to hear."

"And you shared with your team that you were wrong, is that correct?"

"Yes. More than I care to admit."

"So, then answer this—have you felt closer to your team over the past few weeks, or more distant?"

Jonathan had to think about it for a second. Then, amidst all the swirling and stressful thoughts that had been with him all weekend, he remembered those few moments of connection, excitement, and pride they shared in their final meeting with Parth.

"I guess I do feel closer to them. I can't explain it, but something changed once we started having all those conversations."

"And do you sense that your team feels you are more of a leader, or less of a leader because of the actions you've taken over the past few weeks?"

The emotion started quickly, before his mind could connect the dots of what he was actually feeling. Jonathan's eyes started to tear up. It caught him completely off guard. He almost started to panic, before he remembered where he was.

He was thankful that he was in the safety of his own office, and not Helen's conference room.

Yes, he felt closer to his team, and even though the conversations with Parth were difficult at times, it provided a few opportunities for Jonathan to rally them together, in a way that would have felt unnatural before. But Alex and Denise only responded in kind.

They hadn't fixed the problem yet, and honestly, Jonathan knew now that it would be impossible to solve by himself. As much as he wanted to roll up his sleeves, learn about lean startup in detail, and tell everyone what they needed to do, he knew he couldn't. He needed a team, and he wanted the team he had. More importantly, he believed that they trusted him and his leadership.

"Jonathan?" Helen inquired. "Are you still there?"

"Yes." Was the best Jonathan could muster up without letting on that his voice was wavering under everything he was feeling.

"Can you tell me what you are feeling right now?"

Damn, Jonathan thought, *how does she always seem to know what's going on?*

Jonathan composed himself as best he could.

"I think…I'm feeling grateful," Jonathan answered through a broken voice.

"Why are you feeling grateful?"

Jonathan cleared his throat, taking a moment to steady himself.

"Because I can feel that the team *does* see me more as a leader now than, say, six weeks ago. Not because I solved any problems, but, I guess, because I asked for help. I asked *them* for help."

For a moment, Jonathan wished he *was* in the conference room with Helen so he could see her reaction to what he just said. He sensed that she was proud of the progress he had made.

He wondered how a passive invitation from Vaughn could turn into something that had such a significant impact on how he viewed leadership.

"That sounds pretty exciting to me," Helen responded. Even though Jonathan was not in the room with her, he could sense a smile on her face.

Jonathan and Helen spent the rest of the call discussing co-creation and how he could continue to build on the trust he had begun developing with his team.

He remembered telling Amir that he didn't need two coaches and could even remember back when he hesitated to have *one*, but the insights that Parth and Helen provided were very different and equally critical to his success.

They had decided earlier that day that they wanted to continue having Parth coach the team on finding product/market fit through biweekly conference calls and quarterly strategy sessions.

Helen, on the other hand, was helping Jonathan learn how to grow beyond the perfectionist mindset that had made him successful as an engineer and develop the new skills of being a leader. At the end of their call, he went ahead and reaffirmed his commitment to coaching by asking Marsha to put his name on this weekly time slot indefinitely.

20
RIGHT TIME TO SCALE

Jonathan and Vaughn met before sunrise for a hike around Sunset Cliff. They both enjoyed the early morning breeze off the ocean and the picturesque views once the sun came up. It was just a regular morning for Vaughn, but Jonathan couldn't help feeling like a tourist, looking out over the water during sunrise instead of sitting in rush hour traffic. He realized he needed to do this sort of thing more often.

After their hike, they ducked into a nearby coffee shop to catch up on business.

"So, what's the latest on SyncAnalytix? Other than your meetings with Helen—although from what you told me those have been pretty impactful." Vaughn asked as they sat down. "The last time we talked, you were thinking about firing Alex."

"Oh yeah," Jonathan responded as he shook his head in disbelief. He took a sip of his coffee. "It seems like so long ago, now."

"The short answer is that Alex wasn't the problem. Our issue was in customer development. I decided it was a better use of money to put all our resources into finding product/market fit. In the end I canceled the tradeshow. I'm sure you already pieced that together."

"I was wondering which direction things were heading. When we stopped hearing about the tradeshow, though, I figured you must have pivoted," Vaughn said. "I bet that was a hard decision."

Telling the team his decision about the tradeshow had been nerve-wracking, but everything that had happened since then only solidified the fact that it was the right call, to the point where Jonathan nearly forgot how hard it had been.

"Not as hard as I thought, actually," Jonathan explained. He could feel himself smiling, now, as he talked about it.

"That's great." Vaughn looked impressed. "What did the team think?"

"They were a little concerned at first. Some of our staff thought it was a funding issue and that their jobs might be at risk. I made sure to tell them nobody was being let go and walked everyone through my concerns about our current status in the market. It was clear that we needed to delay the launch in Europe until we knew for sure what customer problem we were solving, which needs to start here.

"I probably said some really profound things that I can't remember anymore," Jonathan joked. "Honestly, once the decision was made, I had this sense of...peace... that we were finally heading in the right direction."

"And *are* we heading in the right direction? What do you think?" Vaughn asked.

"Definitely," Jonathan replied. "After I started to meet with Helen, things began to fall into place. Instead of going ahead with the plans for the tradeshow, we took a step back to refocus our efforts on customer discovery. We were able to put forth some new priorities based on what the team came up with by working with Parth, a product/market fit coach."

"A 'product/market fit coach'? I didn't know there was such a thing."

Jonathan thought about the last conversation he'd had with Amir, sitting at a coffee shop like this one. "I didn't know either."

"How did you reorganize the team to focus on product/market fit?" Vaughn asked.

"I guess you could say we shifted the focus from closing sales to solving customer problems," Jonathan began. "A few weeks after we cancelled the tradeshow, our West coast account executive, Mark, resigned. It turned out that he had already accepted another offer and was waiting until after the tradeshow to tell us.

"Anyway, that freed up some budget, so Denise hired a technical product manager."

"What about the rest of the Sales Team?" Vaughn asked. "Are you still unsure about Alex?"

"Alex…" Jonathan paused. He was about to take a sip from his coffee, which he realized he'd been ignoring ever since he first sat down, but he placed his cup back on the table again.

"Well, I'll come back to Alex. First, I want to tell you about Maria, our account executive for the central US. Turns out Maria used to be an application engineer, probably for ten years before switching to sales engineer and eventually account executive. She has a unique expertise we weren't tapping into."

Vaughn raised his eyebrows at that, ready to hear more.

"She's great at helping engineers solve problems, but more important, she listens and asks great questions," Jonathan added. "When she heard what we were doing in customer discovery, she started generating application notes and pulling together customer success stories. In fact, she's written a few blogs for us and presented at an industry meetup last week."

"And Alex?"

"Alex is a rock-star at customer discovery," Jonathan said. "I can't believe I almost let him go. Once we mapped out the plan and how we wanted to refocus, he was all in. We took the time to come to an agreement about our ideal customer and our understanding of their problem. Then we hit the road to talk to customers. All the new intelligence we are gathering is moving us towards validating our assumptions."

"Sounds like Alex is the right fit for SyncAnalytix after all."

"Yes." Jonathan laughed and shook his head. He had been dangerously close to making a huge mistake the last time he and Vaughn sat down together.

"I think when we hired Alex, I had a different role in mind. I thought Alex was supposed to build a national Sales Team, not validate product/market fit. I assumed our product had already been validated in the market and we just needed to hire people to sell it. Of course, I had no analysis or data to back that up, just a gut feeling that it was time to scale the business."

Jonathan paused, shifted his look slightly and said to Vaughn, "It was not the right time to scale."

Vaughn smiled and nodded.

Jonathan continued. "I guess I should have known, especially after two quarters of missed forecasts. If you and Helen hadn't started asking me all those hard questions, I'd probably still be thinking we have a Sales leadership problem."

Vaughn listened the whole time. He looked like he was more than just relieved, but excited for the future of the company. "Sounds like you've had a crazy couple of months," he said. "I could tell there were some obstacles coming up for SyncAnalytix the last time we talked, but I wasn't totally convinced it was in Sales. But you figured it out. So what's next?"

"What's next is I thank you for your help in all of this," Jonathan said, which made Vaughn laugh, and give him a satisfied smile. Jonathan continued, "When we met, I just knew I didn't have a good feeling about Sales, but I didn't know why. You introduced me to Helen who started asking me questions which redirected my focus.

"I realized that what I thought was a Sales problem was actually a product/market fit problem. There was work we needed to do around validating that our product solved a customer problem, *before* we started scaling."

Jonathan paused, thinking of the right way to explain the situation.

"There were a bunch of steps we needed to take before selling the product, so that when we made a sale, we knew it was sustainable. I just assumed that any sales meant the product was ready, but apparently there's a whole demographic of customers who will buy a product before it's ready."

"What kind of customer would do that?"

"Early adopters," Jonathan answered. "Whenever we found one, it felt like we were on the right track with our product. But then they ask you to fix all the stuff that doesn't work perfectly for them. Or, worse, they'll disappear with no explanation."

"Does that explain what happened with LDQ Pipeline?" Vaughn asked. "I remember when we lost them as a customer you said it wasn't a big deal, even though it was ten percent of our revenue at the time."

"Right," Jonathan acknowledged. "I *thought* it was no big deal, but now I see it as an indication of a different issue. We weren't focused on the right things at the time. We should have been focused on metrics that said the product was ready, instead of only looking at sales revenue."

"It sounds like you came across something most CEOs, founders—basically all business owners—struggle with: what to do with the scarce resources that you have," Vaughn explained. "Because what you have is usually not enough to do everything. If you're not deliberate, you waste money. I was suspicious in the last board meeting that the SyncAnalytix strategy wasn't making the most of its available resources."

"Or that we had *no* clear go-to-market strategy to begin with," Jonathan interjected.

Vaughn nodded. "And *no* strategy is almost always the *wrong* strategy. Without a clear strategy, then whatever strategy you may think you're following won't be clear to the rest of your team."

"And then I get the feeling that they're not doing the right things," Jonathan added.

"Exactly. It makes sense that you were considering a personnel change," Vaughn continued. "As the most senior leader in the company, you want to know that you're spending the right money on the right things at the right time."

"I have a feeling you knew the answer to my problem all along."

Vaughn laughed.

"Well, I had some suspicions based on my experience. What you did to get out of that rough patch was all on your own merit—and your team's.

I knew that eventually you would get to the right answer, as long as you were able to think about two other important questions first: Number one, 'Are we spending the right money on the right things at the right time?' and number two, 'Are we doing the right things at the right time to achieve our strategy?', It sounds like that's exactly what you started doing."

"Is it really that easy?" Jonathan asked.

"It can be, sometimes," Vaughn responded. "Think back to your conversations with Helen that you told me about on the trail. She kept asking questions to see if you could convince yourself that you were focusing on the right things."

"Well, at the time it didn't feel simple, even if it sounds like it now," Jonathan said.

Up to this point he'd pretty much accepted that Helen had used some sort of secret, subliminal conversation method to get him pointed in the right direction. But Vaughn had explained it so succinctly that it was starting to make sense.

Jonathan took a deep breath. And a sip of his coffee.

"Well," he said, "since we scheduled this hike, I've been dying to give you a preview of the board meeting next week. I'm excited to share that we're on a path to finding product/market fit with half of the Sales resources. Even though we have a tighter focus on a smaller target market, I feel better about the revenue forecast than I have in a long time."

"That's what I'm talking about!" Vaughn responded. "Congratulations! It's good to hear SyncAnalytix is back on track."

"Thanks. I'm glad that you convinced me to meet with Helen, she's been a big help. I guess it was time I hired an executive coach, after all."

"Well, it's certainly been worth allocating some of my investment to your personal growth," Vaughn added with a smile.

"Oh," Jonathan said, "right."

He and Vaughn both laughed.

"Well," Jonathan started, "now that customer discovery is underway, I'm feeling confident about our ability to find product/market fit. Once we have validated the problem, customer, and channel, it will be *time to scale*," he finished as he raised his coffee cup with confidence.

Vaughn also raised his cup to toast Jonathan's success. "To finding product/market fit," he concluded.

STARTUP RESOURCES

Ursache, Marius. 2019. "Problem Statement Canvas for Startups and Innovation Teams." Metabeta. March 27, 2019. https://www.metabeta.com/articles/process/problem-statement-canvas/.

> This is where every entrepreneur needs to start. Before you specify a product, start development, or meet with customers, first articulate what you believe about the problem you solve. The *Problem Statement Canvas* provides an excellent framework for capturing what you know about the problem and a method for uncovering the opportunity that may exist and the competitive advantage you can create.

Fitzpatrick, Rob. 2013. *The Mom Test: How to Talk to Customers & Learn If Your Business Is a Good Idea When Everyone Is Lying to You.* North Charleston, SC: Createspace Independent Publishing Platform.

> If you are an engineer, anyone not used to talking with customers, or a founder who can't stop talking about their product long enough to understand a customer's real problem, you definitely need this book. *The Mom Test* is a great resource for how to engage customers in a discussion about the problem they face.

Schwartzfarb, Amos. 2021. *Sell More Faster: The Ultimate Sales Playbook for Start-Ups.* Gildan Media Corporation.

> *Sell More Faster* is a structured approach to defining who you are selling to. It applies some lean startup concepts and provides resources to help the reader understand the basics of early-stage startup sales.

Blank, Steven Gary. 2005. *The Four Steps to the Epiphany: Successful Strategies for Products That Win.* 3rd ed. K & S Ranch Consulting.

> Steve Blank's book formed the basis for what has become a

movement. The book is rich with information about Customer Development, but may be, at times, overwhelming.

Ries, Eric. 2011. *The Lean Startup*. New York, NY: Crown Publishing Group.

> Eric Ries' book took the concepts of customer development first presented by Steve Blank and made them easier to understand. With his easy-to-read writing style and personal examples, Eric created the perfect book to present a new way for technology entrepreneurs to think about their startup.

Furr, Nathan, and Paul Ahlstrom. 2011. *Nail It Then Scale It: The Entrepreneur's Guide to Creating and Managing Breakthrough Innovation*. Nisi Institute.

> *Nail It Then Scale It* is a practical guide to applying lean startup concepts. It combines high-level principles, and a step-by-step guide of what key actions successful entrepreneurs take to reduce risk and increase success. For additional resources- https://www.nailthenscale.com/.

Maurya, Ash. 2022. *Running Lean: Iterate from Plan A to a Plan That Works*. 3rd ed. Sebastopol, CA: O'Reilly Media.

> *Running Lean* is a practical guide to applying ideas and concepts from lean startup, business model design, design thinking, and jobs-to-be-done. In addition to presenting a step-by-step example, Ash also introduces the Lean Canvas. For additional resources- https://leanstack.com/

Parker, Dave. 2021. *Trajectory: Startup: Ideation to Product/Market Fit*. BenBella Books.

> In addition to being an indispensable resource which covers the full entrepreneurial journey, chapter 11 of *Trajectory: Startup* presents fourteen business models along with recommended metrics to track.

Moore, Geoffrey A. 1995. *Inside the Tornado: Marketing Strategies from Silicon Valley's Cutting Edge*. United Kingdom: HarperCollins.
> Geoffrey presents the chasm model and bowling alley market development strategy. Geoffrey's description of being 'inside the tornado' is very similar if not fundamental to the definition of product/market fit.

Moore, Geoffrey. 1999. *Crossing the Chasm*. New York, NY: HarperBusiness.
> Geoffrey presents his basic theory on the dynamics of early markets and market development strategy. He also walks the reader through target-customer characterization with an illustrative example of 'A Day in the Life'.

Cleveland, Bruce, and Wildcat Venture Partners. 2019. *Traversing the Traction Gap*. New York, NY: Diversion Books.
> Bruce and his partners at Wildcat Ventures expanded on the chasm model and bowling alley market development first introduced by Geoffrey Moore.

Eric Ries, 2017. *The Startup Way: How Entrepreneurial Management Transforms Culture and Drives Growth*. London, England: Portfolio Penguin.
> *The Startup Way*, goes further in describing the concepts and providing more generic applications of lean startup processes to a corporate setting. It shows how to apply the concepts more generically and provides examples which are easy for the reader to follow.

Lencioni, P. M. 2020. *The Motive - Why so Many Leaders Abdicate Their Most Important Responsibilities*. Nashville, TN: John Wiley & Sons.
> *The Motive* is a leadership fable about how to be a connected CEO. The book does a great job presenting a situation where an entitled CEO thinks he is leading his company but has abdicated his leadership – instead believing he is CEO because he deserves it.

Blank, Steve, and Bob Dorf. 2020. *The Startup Owner's Manual the Startup Owner's Manual: The Step-by-Step Guide for Building a Great Company.* Nashville, TN: John Wiley & Sons.

> *The Startup Owner's Manual*® is an updated and more concise version of Steve Blank's original book. It covers the first two stages of Customer Development – Customer Discovery and Customer Validation. The best practices, lessons, and tips found in the book are a great resource for entrepreneurs. Some of the original concepts from *The Four Steps to the Epiphany* have been updated and expanded in this newer version.

Feld, Brad, and Jason Mendelson. 2017. *Venture Deals: Be Smarter than Your Lawyer and Venture Capitalist.* 3rd ed. Nashville, TN: John Wiley & Sons.

> This is a great resource for entrepreneurs who are unfamiliar with the typical terms around fundraising.

Wasserman, Noam. 2021. *The Founder's Dilemmas the Founder's Dilemmas: Anticipating and Avoiding the Pitfalls That Can Sink a Startup.* Princeton, NJ: Princeton University Press.

> This is a great resource for entrepreneurs who are unfamiliar with the typical terms around entrepreneurship in general such as equity ownership.

Glaser, Judith E. 2016. *Conversational Intelligence: How Great Leaders Build Trust and Get Extraordinary Results.* Routledge.

Cohn, Alisa. 2021. *From Start-up to Grown-up: Grow Your Leadership to Grow Your Business.* London, England: Kogan Page.

Osterwalder, Alexander, and Yves Pigneur. 2013. *Business Model Generation: A Handbook for Visionaries, Game Changers, and Challengers.* 1st ed. Chichester, England: John Wiley & Sons.

Christensen, Clayton M. 2016. *The Innovator's Dilemma: When New Technologies Cause Great Firms to Fail.* Boston, MA: Harvard Business Review Press.

Christensen, Clayton M., and Michael E. Raynor. 2013. *The Innovator's Solution: Creating and Sustaining Successful Growth*. Boston, MA: Harvard Business Review Press.

Christensen, Clayton M., Taddy Hall, Karen Dillon, and David S. Duncan. 2016. *Competing against Luck: The Story of Innovation and Customer Choice*. HarperBusiness.

Doerr, John. 2018. *Measure What Matters: OKRs: The Simple Idea That Drives 10x Growth*. London, England: Portfolio Penguin.

Croll, Alistair. 2013. *Lean Analytics: Use Data to Build a Better Startup Faster*. Sebastopol, CA: O'Reilly Media.

NOTES

Foreword

ii   Blank, Steve. 2013. "Why the Lean Start-up Changes
Everything." Harvard Business Review, May 1, 2013.
https://hbr.org/2013/05/why-the-lean-start-up-changes-
everything

Chapter 1
Fire the VP

2   Internet-of-Things (IoT) describes physical objects (or
groups of such objects) with sensors, processing ability,
software, and other technologies that connect and exchange
data with other devices and systems over the Internet or
other communications networks. Wikipedia contributors.
2022. "Internet of Things." Wikipedia, The Free
Encyclopedia.
https://en.wikipedia.org/w/index.php?title=Internet_of_thi
ngs

2   ZigBee® is a low-power, low data rate, and close proximity
(i.e., personal area) wireless ad hoc network based on IEEE
802.15.4. ZigBee® is a registered trademark of the ZigBee
Alliance. Wikipedia contributors. 2022. "Zigbee." Wikipedia,
The Free Encyclopedia.
https://en.wikipedia.org/w/index.php?title=Zigbee

6   MVP refers to a Minimum Viable Product. "It's a concise
summary of the smallest possible group of features that will
work as a stand-alone product while still solving at least the
"core" problem and demonstrating the product's value."
Blank, Steve., Dorf, Bob. *The Startup Owner's Manual: The*

Step-By-Step Guide for Building a Great Company. United Kingdom: Wiley, 2020. p. 80

6   The goal of Customer Discovery is "finding out who the customers for your product are and whether the problem you believe you are solving is important to them." Blank, Steven Gary. *The Four Steps to the Epiphany: Successful Strategies for Products that Win.* Germany: S.G. Blank, 2007. p. 20

6   Conversational Intelligence® is a registered trademark of The CreatingWE® Institute. "Conversational Intelligence is essential to an organization's ability to create shared meaning about what needs to be accomplished and why, so that employees get excited and are clear about the future they are helping to create." Glaser, Judith E.. *Conversational Intelligence: How Great Leaders Build Trust and Get Extraordinary Results.* N.p.: Taylor & Francis, 2016. p. xxi

Chapter 2
Forecast Review

9   The goal of forecast review meetings is to go through and understand the deals that make up the current period's forecast. The concepts related to forecast reviews and pipeline meetings are drawn from the *Sales Forecasts: A Question of Method Not Magic* (OpenView Venture Partners, 2012) https://openviewpartners.com/wp-content/uploads/2012/07/Forecasting-eBook-FINAL.pdf

10   The aim of a pipeline review is to monitor the health of the overall pipeline, not just the deals in the current forecast. *Sales Forecasts: A Question of Method Not Magic.* p.22

Chapter 3
Marketing

16   The term TechnoLatin refers to "vague but precise-sounding words that work like the blank tiles in Scrabble: you can use

them anywhere, but they have no value." Locke, Christopher., Weinberger, David., Levine, Rick., Searls, Doc. *The Cluetrain Manifesto: 10th Anniversary Edition.* United States: Basic Books, 2011. p. 176

Chapter 4
Conversational IQ

20   The term shared meaning or sense making refers to Level III transformational conversations where we "co-create and partner in creating a shared reality". Glaser, Judith E.. *Conversational Intelligence: How Great Leaders Build Trust and Get Extraordinary Results.* N.p.: Taylor & Francis, 2016. pp. 91-92

21   Questions and answers derived from an interview of Judith Glaser by Alan Steinfeld. NewRealities. 2013. "Judith E. Glaser Talks about Conversational Intelligence." Youtube. November 19, 2013. https://www.youtube.com/watch?v=fPrwizcRunA.

Chapter 6
Customer Discovery

43   Ries, Eric. *The Lean Startup: How Today's Entrepreneurs Use Continuous Innovation to Create Radically Successful Businesses.* United Kingdom: Crown, 2011.

44   "The movement that is transforming how new products are built and launched." http://theleanstartup.com/

44   Customer Development is a process distinct from Product Development where the focus is to learn and discover who the company's initial customers will be and what markets they are in. Blank, Steven Gary. *The Four Steps to the Epiphany: Successful Strategies for Products that Win.* Germany: S.G. Blank, 2007. p. 15

45   The goal of Customer Validation is "to build a repeatable sales road map for the sales and marketing teams." Blank, Steven Gary. *The Four Steps to the Epiphany: Successful Strategies for Products that Win.* Germany: S.G. Blank, 2007. p. 21

45   The most common model for bringing a new product to market in the 20th century. "The new-product introduction model is a good fit for an existing company where the customers are well known, the product features can be spec'ed upfront, the market is well-defined, and the basis of competition is understood." Blank, Steve., Dorf, Bob. *The Startup Owner's Manual: The Step-By-Step Guide for Building a Great Company.* United Kingdom: Wiley, 2020. pp. 2-7

46   Blank, Steve. 2013. "Why the Lean Start-up Changes Everything." Harvard Business Review, May 1, 2013. https://hbr.org/2013/05/why-the-lean-start-up-changes-everything.

Chapter 7
Lean Startup

51   Ries, Eric. *The Lean Startup: How Today's Entrepreneurs Use Continuous Innovation to Create Radically Successful Businesses.* United Kingdom: Crown, 2011.

51   Blank, Steven Gary. *The Four Steps to the Epiphany: Successful Strategies for Products that Win.* Germany: S.G. Blank, 2005.

52   The Customer Development Model contains four easy-to-understand steps: customer discovery, customer validation, customer creation, and company building. Blank, Steven Gary. *The Four Steps to the Epiphany: Successful Strategies for Products that Win.* Germany: S.G. Blank, 2005. p. 19

53   Adapted from the four phases of Customer Discovery. Blank, Steve., Dorf, Bob. *The Startup Owner's Manual: The*

Step-By-Step Guide for Building a Great Company. United Kingdom: Wiley, 2020. pp. 67-68

54   Adapted from the Phase 1: State your Hypotheses. Blank, Steven Gary. *The Four Steps to the Epiphany: Successful Strategies for Products that Win.* Germany: S.G. Blank, 2005. p. 40

55   "...there's nothing worse than spending years in a startup only to discover that it can never grow to more than a few million dollars in revenue..." Blank, Steve., Dorf, Bob. *The Startup Owner's Manual: The Step-By-Step Guide for Building a Great Company.* United Kingdom: Wiley, 2020. p. 71

56   From the State Your Hypotheses: The Product. Blank, Steven Gary. *The Four Steps to the Epiphany: Successful Strategies for Products that Win.* Germany: S.G. Blank, 2005. p. 41

57   Validated learning is "learning based on real data gathering rather than guesses about the future". Ries, Eric. *The Startup Way: How Modern Companies Use Entrepreneurial Management to Transform Culture and Drive Long-Term Growth.* United States: Crown, 2017. p. 96

58   An archive of the best articles from Marc Andreessen's 2007 blog. Kin, Fictive. n.d. "Pmarchive · The Only Thing That Matters." Pmarchive.com. https://pmarchive.com/guide_to_startups_part4.html.

60   The 9 Deadly Sins of the New Product Introduction Model. Blank, Steve., Dorf, Bob. *The Startup Owner's Manual: The Step-By-Step Guide for Building a Great Company.* United Kingdom: Wiley, 2020. pp. 8-18

Chapter 8
Deadly Sins

67   "The New Product Introduction Model is a good fit for an existing company where the customers are known, the

product features can be spec'd upfront, the market is well-defined, and the basis of competition is understood." Blank, Steve., Dorf, Bob. *The Startup Owner's Manual: The Step-By-Step Guide for Building a Great Company.* United Kingdom: Wiley, 2020. p. 3

72   Shifting from I to WE. Glaser, Judith E.. *Conversational Intelligence: How Great Leaders Build Trust and Get Extraordinary Results.* N.p.: Taylor & Francis, 2016. pp. 56-57

Chapter 9
Staying Connected

80   "The idea of the chasm is a simple one. It says that whenever truly innovative high-tech products are first brought to market, they will initially enjoy a warm welcome in an early market made up of technology enthusiasts and visionaries but then will fall into a chasm, during which sales falter and often plummet." Moore, Geoffrey A.. *Inside the Tornado: Marketing Strategies from Silicon Valley's Cutting Edge.* United Kingdom: HarperCollins, 1995. pp. 19-20

Chapter 11
Fifteen Minutes

98   A value-added reseller (VAR) is a company that adds features or services to an existing product, then resells it (usually to end-users) as an integrated product or complete "turn-key" solution. Wikipedia contributors. (2021, November 1). *Value-added reseller.* Wikipedia, The Free Encyclopedia. https://en.wikipedia.org/w/index.php?title=Value-added_reseller&oldid=1052961599

Chapter 12
Market

109   "Wireless IoT Sensors Market by Type, Size, Growth and
       Forecast – 2027." n.d. Marketresearchfuture.com.
       https://www.marketresearchfuture.com/reports/wireless-
       iot-sensors-market-8269.

110   "Industrial Wireless Sensor Network Market Share Report,
       2025." n.d. Grandviewresearch.com.
       https://www.grandviewresearch.com/industry-
       analysis/industrial-wireless-sensor-networks-iwsn-market.

Chapter 13
Problem

115   The discussion around the problem was derived from the
       article by Marius Ursache about the problem statement
       canvas. Ursache, Marius. 2019. "Problem Statement Canvas
       for Startups and Innovation Teams." Metabeta. March 27,
       2019.
       https://www.metabeta.com/articles/process/problem-
       statement-canvas/

134   Whirlwind – everything that must be accomplished in the
       course of day-to-day work. Huling, Jim., McChesney, Chris.,
       Covey, Sean. *The 4 Disciplines of Execution: Achieving Your
       Wildly Important Goals.* United States: Simon & Schuster,
       2021. p. 31

Chapter 14
Customer

136   The discussion around 'Ready', 'Willing', 'Able', and 'Made
       successful' was derived from the Lean B2B blog about "How
       to Create An Ideal Customer Profile in B2B – Examples &
       Templates". N.d. Leanb2bbook.com.

https://leanb2bbook.com/blog/how-create-ideal-customer-profile-b2b-customer-development/.

141　Theory of Constraints. Goldratt, Eliyahu M.., Goldratt, EM.., Cox, Jeff. *The Goal: A Process of Ongoing Improvemnt*. United Kingdom: North River Press, 1992.

142　"In Customer Development, the *founders gather firsthand experience about every component of the business model. The team can support the founders, but firsthand experience by definition cannot be delegated*." –and– "Founders Must Lead the Customer Validation Team". Blank, Steve., Dorf, Bob. *The Startup Owner's Manual: The Step-By-Step Guide for Building a Great Company*. United Kingdom: Wiley, 2020. pp. 31-32, 283

143　The day-in-the-life discussion was derived from the Chapter 4 of *Crossing the Chasm* "Target the Point of Attack". Moore, Geoffrey A.. *Crossing the Chasm*. United Kingdom: HarperCollins, 1999. pp. 96-99

Chapter 15
Product

148　"The lesson is simple: start with the problem space, and you will end up with more effective solutions." Partners, Wildcat Venture., Cleveland, Bruce. *Traversing the Traction Gap*. United States: Radius Book Group, 2019. p. 112

149　"The "market pull" approach attempts to provide products the market demands. The "technology push" approach attempts to interest the market in new products based on new solutions." Dixon, Jon. 2001. "The Market Pull Versus Technology Push Continuum Of Engineering Education." *Proceedings of the 2001 American Society for Engineering Education Annual Conference & Exposition*.

153　"To dominate a segment typically means winning 40 percent or more of its new business over the past year to eighteen months." Moore, Geoffrey A.. *Inside the Tornado: Marketing Strategies from Silicon Valley's Cutting Edge.* United Kingdom: HarperCollins, 1995. p. 44

154 "…pragmatist customers *expect* to buy the market leading product." Moore, Geoffrey A.. *Inside the Tornado: Marketing Strategies from Silicon Valley's Cutting Edge.* United Kingdom: HarperCollins, 1995. p. 32

154 No market need "Tackling problems that are interesting to solve rather than those that serve a market need was cited as the No. 2 reason for failure, noted in 35% of cases." Insights, C. B. 2021. "Why Startups Fail: Top 12 Reasons 1 CB Insights." CB Insights Research. CB Insights. August 3, 2021. https://www.cbinsights.com/research/startup-failure-reasons-top/.

157 "Visionaries are that rare breed of people who have the insight to match an emerging technology to a strategic opportunity, the temperament to translate that insight into a high-visibility, high-risk project, and the charisma to get the rest of their organization to buy into that project. They are the early adopters of high-tech products." Moore, Geoffrey A.. *Crossing the Chasm.* United Kingdom: HarperCollins, 1999. pp. 33-34

157 Moore, Geoffrey A.. *Crossing the Chasm: marketing and selling technology products to mainstream customers.* New York: HarperBusiness, 1991.

157 "The adoption of an innovation usually follows a normal, bell-shaped curve when plotted over time on a frequency basis." Rogers, Everett M.. *Diffusion of Innovations*, 5th Edition. United Kingdom: Free Press, 2003. p. 272

158 Graphic derived from "Introducing the Chasm". Moore, Geoffrey A.. *Inside the Tornado: Marketing Strategies from Silicon*

Valley's Cutting Edge. United Kingdom: HarperCollins, 1995. pp. 18-19

158   "...visionaries are easy to sell but very hard to please." Moore, Geoffrey A.. *Crossing the Chasm.* United Kingdom: HarperCollins, 1999. p. 35

160   "*The Tornado,* a period of mass-market adoption, when the general marketplace switches over to the new infrastructure paradigm." Moore, Geoffrey A.. *Inside the Tornado: Marketing Strategies from Silicon Valley's Cutting Edge.* United Kingdom: HarperCollins, 1995. p. 25

Chapter 16
Discovery

167   Get Ready to Sell: Hire a Sales Closer. "A sales closer is not a VP of Sales who wants to immediately build and manage a large sales organization. A sales closer is someone with a great Rolodex in the market you are selling into." Blank, Steven Gary. *The Four Steps to the Epiphany: Successful Strategies for Products that Win.* Germany: S.G. Blank, 2005. p. 99

171   Adapted from The Story of Spanning – "the project became a product, the product became a company.". Wood, Charlie. 2018. "The Story of Spanning." Youtube. December 14, 2018. https://www.youtube.com/watch?v=u5icEXWpDmg.

172   Adapted from questions found in the section Have We Found a Product/Market Fit?. Blank, Steve., Dorf, Bob. *The Startup Owner's Manual: The Step-By-Step Guide for Building a Great Company.* United Kingdom: Wiley, 2020. pp. 260-264

172   Lean Canvas is an adaptation of the Business Model Canvas®. Maurya, Ash. *Running Lean: Iterate from Plan A to a Plan That Works.* Germany: O'Reilly Media, Incorporated, 2012. p. 5

Chapter 17
Learn

178   Build-Measure-Learn feedback loop. Ries, Eric. *The Startup Way: How Modern Companies Use Entrepreneurial Management to Transform Culture and Drive Long-Term Growth.* United States: Crown, 2017. pp. 105-107

180   Adding Hypotheses and Insights to Build-Measure-Learn adapted from The Customer Development Insight Cycle, Figure 2.3. Blank, Steve., Dorf, Bob. *The Startup Owner's Manual: The Step-By-Step Guide for Building a Great Company.* United Kingdom: Wiley, 2020. p. 38

181   "Start the MVP Brief by defining what needs to be learned— and from whom.". Blank, Steve., Dorf, Bob. *The Startup Owner's Manual: The Step-By-Step Guide for Building a Great Company.* United Kingdom: Wiley, 2020. p. 80

191   Barlow, Buckley. 2016. "The Bow Tie Funnel: How Forward-Thinking Organizations Optimize for Growth." In The Know. BeInTheKnow. October 19, 2016. https://beintheknow.co/bow-tie-funnel/.

Chapter 18
Leaps

193   Leap-of-faith assumptions are "the beliefs about what must be true in order for the startup to succeed." Ries, Eric. *The Startup Way: How Modern Companies Use Entrepreneurial Management to Transform Culture and Drive Long-Term Growth.* United States: Crown, 2017. p. 86

198   Four-quadrant matrix adapted from the figure titled PRIORITIZING LEAP-OF-FAITH ASSUMPTIUONS. Ries, Eric. *The Startup Way: How Modern Companies Use Entrepreneurial Management to Transform Culture and Drive Long-Term Growth.* United States: Crown, 2017. p. 93

200 Leap Scoring Chart adapted from the figure titled MVP
SCORING CHART. Ries, Eric. *The Startup Way: How Modern
Companies Use Entrepreneurial Management to Transform Culture
and Drive Long-Term Growth.* United States: Crown, 2017. p.
102

ACKNOWLEDGMENTS

I want to start off by acknowledging my co-author Kathryn Eversmann. I had the story rolling around in my mind for a long time before I was able to turn it into a very, very rough first draft. I sent that draft, and all the other ramblings I had, to her, and she began working her magic (as I like to say). Instead of clunky dialogue and a storyline that was hard to visualize, she gave life to the characters and made the story flow. After reading her first round of edits, I thought to myself, *wow, we might really be able to create something here.* She went on to work her magic on eleven subsequent drafts of this book, and if it weren't for her ability to show me how effective my writing could be, I doubt this book would have made it past that first draft.

I also want to give special thanks to reviewers who took their time to read the rough drafts and provide valuable feedback. First to Robert Jones, who read draft #4 and recommended that I take the management lessons and move them into the storyline. To Hillary Skaff who provided chapter by chapter editorial feedback of draft #4. To Alicia Marie who provided encouragement and feedback on the executive coach character, Helen (along with some thoughts on the other characters) in draft #6.

To Ada Ryland for providing feedback on draft #8 and agreeing to write the Foreword. I feel honored to be partnering with Ada to help entrepreneurs navigate their way to product/market fit. To Ilyas Iyoob who provided technical feedback on the analytics material in draft #9 and to Ben Allen, Dale Wilson, and Amir Arad who also provided feedback on draft #9. To Dean Dzurilla who provided detailed feedback from an entrepreneur's perspective on draft #7, spent hours discussing the concepts, and provided a lot of encouragement as I worked through the remaining revisions. And finally, to Grant Shillings who edited the final version.

I would also like to acknowledge Catherine Covington and Dr. Elise Brazier. It was a lunch meeting with Catherine in 2017 that first gave me the idea for a series of books to present founder challenges in a relatable story. I value our discussions and friendship over the years. Dr. Brazier offered me the opportunity to teach entrepreneurship at Concordia University. The content of this book has changed dramatically over the past two years as I have taught and tested different lean startup concepts with the MBA cohorts I have had the privilege of working with.

Finally, I want to thank my life partner and biggest supporter, Dori Eversmann. After I finished the first draft, Dori was the first to read it and encouraged me along the way, even when I would get stuck for months at a time, trying to work concepts out in my head before putting them down on paper. So many chapters have changed since that first draft, and so many chapters are new, that I cannot wait for her to read the final version.

ABOUT THE AUTHORS

Jeff Eversmann is a Product/Market Fit Coach, co-founder and General Partner of Long View Technology Ventures, the CFO of Long View Equity, and an Adjunct Instructor at Concordia University Texas. He has been working with technology startups since 1994. Prior to co-founding Long View Technology Ventures, Jeff worked as a fractional CFO for multiple startups in Austin, Texas. His expertise includes new product development, finance, and entrepreneurship, including fundraising, strategy, and launching new companies. He has degrees in management and engineering from the Georgia Institute of Technology in Atlanta, Georgia along with an MBA in Entrepreneurship from the Acton School of Business in Austin, Texas.

Fooled by Early Adopters, Jeff's debut novel, was inspired by his years of experience working in and around early-stage startups along with teaching entrepreneurship based on lean startup concepts to MBA students. The story was written with the goal of providing simple tools for finding product/market fit while alerting founders to common mistakes that often result in product failures due to 'no market need'.

More information about Jeff and finding product/market fit can be found at *www.jeffeversmann.com*

Kathryn Eversmann is a freelance writer and editor. The most rewarding aspect of her work is the moment when a client discovers their own capabilities for communication and self-expression. Kathryn has lived and studied internationally, most recently in Wrocław, Poland, where she completed a degree in cultural studies. Her writing has been recognized in a variety of fields.